HIGHER
FASTER
LONGER

*My Life in Aviation
and My Quest for Spaceflight*

By WALLY FUNK
As told to LORETTA HALL
Foreword by EILEEN COLLINS

©2020 by Loretta Hall
All rights reserved.

No part of this book may be used or reproduced by any means: graphic, electronic, or mechanical, including photocopying, recording, taping or by any information storage retrieval system without the written permission of the author except in the case of brief quotations embodied in critical articles and reviews. Because of the dynamic nature of the Internet, any web addresses or links contained in this book may have changed since publication and may no longer be valid. Although every precaution has been taken to verify the accuracy of the information contained herein, the author and publisher assume no responsibility for any errors or omissions so that no liability is assumed for damages that may result from the use of information contained within. The views expressed in this work are solely those of the author and do not necessarily reflect the views of the publisher whereby the publisher hereby disclaims any responsibility for them.

ORDERING BOOKS FOR QUANTITY SALES
Special discounts are available on quantity purchases by corporations, associations, and others. For details, contact the author's publicist at the following URL: www.wallyfly.com/ContactWally.html

ATTRIBUTIONS
Interior Text Font: Minion Pro
Interior Title Fonts: Minion Pro
Editor: Sharilyn Grayson
Cover Design: Robbie Grayson
Photo Courtesies: Wally Funk, M. Parker

TRAiTMARKER BOOKS
2984 Del Rio Pike
Franklin, TN 37069
traitmarkerbooks.com
traitmarker@gmail.com

ISBN: 978-1-64970-461-0
(also an ebook on Amazon.com)

A *Space Traveler Book*s imprint

Printed in the United States of America

*To my mother, Virginia Shy Funk.
She was a kind and gentle mother, a model
of politeness and positivity. She encouraged my curiosity and
accepted my interests in traditionally male activities despite
her own genteel upbringing. When I was a child, I learned
from her example of helping others through community
activities. When I became an adult, she happily shared
my more adventurous activities.
Thank you, Little Momma.*

5 Star Reviews

✶✶✶✶✶

for *Higher, Faster, Longer*

Open Air has great passion for inspiring aviation in today's youth, especially women. Wally Funk, Loretta, and the ladies of Mercury 13 personify the greatness of that purpose. This is a must read!

Jeffrey L. 'JJ' Jorgenson, CFI, CFII, Multi
2019 Minnesota Aviation Hall of Fame Book Award
Author of *Open Air*

Higher, Faster, Longer *is a truly inspirational book. Not only is it interesting but demonstrates the value of education, determination, and persistence in achieving worthwhile goals. It will be a shining example, especially for young women, to achieve their dreams in aviation and space for the coming many decades. I highly recommend the book for your reading pleasure.*

Carl G. Schneider, Major General, USAF (Ret)
Author of *Jet Pioneer*

Wally Funk's life and indefatigable spirit are a testament to her passion for life, aviation, and all things UP! She is energy, focus, and positivity personified. Wally is a soul as self-assured and self-possessed as any human you will ever meet. She has incorporated her love of the Taos mountains and all the wisdom that they embody in her hypersonic life. Dauntless. Fearless. Intrepid. Wally is spark and spunk and walks always with her eyes turned upward. Loretta Hall has written a book celebrating this living legend whose daringness has opened doors for women in aviation and continues to inspire all who hear her story. Wally Funk...a smile, a vitality, and a heart as wide as the world itself.

JANET IVEY, PRESIDENT, EXPLORE MARS, INC.
CEO JANET'S PLANET, INC.

I have had the privilege of meeting Wally many years ago and was impressed with her initiative, knowledge, and friendly nature. Now, through the pages of her biography, I have had the opportunity to follow her amazing life through the skies and her exploits around the world. All who have the occasion to read her story will be enthralled by this very special person. I especially recommend it to young women considering career directions, because it shows what a person can achieve when they have a dedicated goal and work to overcome gender biases.

TED SPITZMILLER
AEROSPACE HISTORIAN
AUTHOR OF *THE HISTORY OF HUMAN SPACE FLIGHT*

If I was ever asked to name ten of the most enthralling people I have ever met – and I have met literally thousands in the aerospace/

spaceflight arena – Wally Funk would have to be one of the first I would nominate. Every moment of her life is spent in a restless state of excitement and adventure, and always with anticipation for whatever lies ahead. She has had a positive impact on so many lives, and is thrilled when that impact comes back to her in the form of young people wanting to emulate her flying achievements. I can recall driving from Dallas to the small Texas town of Quanah with Wally, where I was doing a book launch involving local astronaut Ed Givens, and she was giving talks at a couple of schools. Wally was truly excited the whole road trip, even though she has given her talk at literally dozens of schools and other institutions over many years, and a long trip in miles was all too short in hours as Wally and I traded stories. She has told me what it was like undergoing and passing those Mercury astronaut tests at the Lovelace Clinic in New Mexico all those decades back, which is a truly remarkable episode in America's early days of astronautics. Wally Funk is not only one of the most delightful and interesting people one could ever hope to meet, but a genuine inspiration. What she has achieved in her lifetime is extraordinary, and even though Wally and I have met several times, I still find endless fascination in learning more about her life and exploits. I look forward to this new book with great anticipation. Wally Funk is, and always will be, a person I not only admire but regard as a modern-day champion and legend of aviation and spaceflight history.

COLIN BURGESS
AUTHOR OF SELECTING THE MERCURY SEVEN: THE SEARCH FOR
AMERICA'S FIRST ASTRONAUTS & SHATTERED DREAMS: THE LOST
OR CANCELED SPACE MISSIONS

Table of Contents

Foreword — i
Introduction — v

Chapter 1: The Fascination Begins — 1
   Supergirl — 1
   Call Me Wally — 5
   Throw It a Fish — 8
   Adventurous — 11

Chapter 2: I Sprout Wings — 17
   Stephens College — 17
   Let's Try Something Else — 20
   Taking Flight — 22
   Flying Is Freedom — 25

Chapter 3: I Want Some Space — 33
   Potential Lady Orbiter — 33
   Lovelace — 36
   You're Better Than That — 41
   Patience — 47

Chapter 4: My Quest Continues — 51
   Not Finished Testing — 51
   I Set a Record — 54

The Wally Funk Program	*57*
El Toro Testing	*62*
Gravity at USC	*64*

Chapter 5: Adventures on Three Continents — 67
Europe	*67*
Middle East	*76*
Africa	*77*
Back on the Road	*82*

Chapter 6: I Look at Flight from Both Sides Now — 89
Amazing America	*89*
First Lady Inspector at the FAA	*91*
First Lady Investigator at the NTSB	*96*
Unpredictable	*101*
Patterns	*107*

Chapter 7: Freedom and Independence — 113
At Home in Taos	*113*
Chief Pilot Again	*118*
Off to the Races	*122*
A Royal Presence	*126*
The Taos Kid	*131*

Chapter 8: Don't Let Your Last Flight Be Your Last Flight
The Wally Stick	*137*
How to Fly and Stay Alive	*139*
A Wing Against the Sky	*148*

Chapter 9: Ninety-Nine Reasons to Travel		153
   India		*153*
   China		*159*
   Russia		*165*
   Flying High		*169*

Chapter 10: Detours on the Way to Space		173
   The Space Community		*173*
   Training for Space		*176*
   Space Pilot Eileen Collins		*178*
   Star City		*183*

Chapter 11: She's Got a Ticket to Fly		193
   Space Adventures		*193*
   Wally's Ticket to Space		*194*
   Virgin Galactic		*199*
   This Kid Has No Regrets		*204*

To the Reader: Notes for Context		207
The Mercury 13		225
Resources		229
Index		233
Acknowledgments		239
About the Authors		241
Wally's Awards		243

Foreword

A few months after receiving my first assignment to fly a space shuttle mission, the public relations people at NASA relayed an invitation to me. A group of women known as the Mercury 13 were meeting with a Hollywood producer who wanted to film a documentary about their previously unknown experiences. I hadn't heard of these women before, but I learned that in the early 1960s they had passed the same medical and physiological tests as the Mercury 7 astronauts. The women worked to convince NASA to accept them as astronaut candidates, but they weren't eligible. NASA required the candidates to be military test pilots, a field that was only open to men at that time.

I also learned that they took those grueling, week-long tests alone or with only one other woman. Other than those who had a testing partner, they had never met each other. This 1994 meeting would be their first time to get acquainted. They also wanted to meet me because I was training to be the first female pilot of a NASA spaceflight—something they had aspired to. When I heard their amazing story, I eagerly accepted their invitation.

Two of the Mercury 13 had died by that time, and two weren't able to come to the gathering. But I met the other nine. They were fascinating people. The youngest one was a dynamo named Wally Funk. I'm happy to see that Wally is finally telling her story through this book.

I remember how energetic and highly motivated Wally

was then, and still is. Back in 1961, these female pilots' efforts to become America's first spacewomen came to a dead end. Wally managed to move through that disappointment and go on to accomplish great things in her life. She became an inspiring role model for women in aviation. She has a contagious love for flying and for the people in the aviation community. As the first female investigator for the National Transportation Safety Board (NTSB), Wally took on a very, very tough job and did it courageously and competently. She seems to have poured her heart and soul into her love of aviation and sharing it with others. And she never gave up her desire to go into space. She wanted to go farther than she could go in an airplane. When I met her, Wally still believed she would fly in space someday. She would find a way to make it happen. She's still trying.

Wally has the spirit of an explorer. She wants to go places, meet people, and learn new things. She wants to learn more about airplanes, how they work, how they fly, the kinds of missions they do, the kind of people that fly. Her continuing desire to fly in space is part of her explorer nature. She wants to learn more about the world that we live in, the environment that airplanes fly in, and the environment that spacecraft fly in.

I suspect that part of her desire to fly in space may be to finish the job that the Mercury 13 started. Six decades ago, they were stymied in their efforts to become astronauts because they were women. I can relate in a small way to that experience. I remember going to my local airport when I was twenty years old to ask for flying lessons and being afraid they would say no because I was a girl. Later, in 1978, I was thrilled to be accepted into pilot training in the Air Force only two years after women became eligible for such training. But I still couldn't fly my dream airplanes—the F-104, 105, and 106—because in those days, women were prohibited, by federal law, from flying combat aircraft. It wasn't until 1993 that the combat restriction was finally lifted.

In 1990, I was selected as the first woman to train as a pilot astronaut in the space shuttle program. It took many years for NASA to get to that point, but I believe the Mercury 13 helped make it happen. They had demonstrated years earlier that women had the physical endurance and aptitude to perform as astronauts.

It's my hope that Wally can fulfill her dream of launching into space with Virgin Galactic and also fulfill the goal of all the Mercury 13, which was to prove that women could be successful space explorers. I've heard that Wally performed better than John Glenn on at least one of the original astronaut qualifying tests. Glenn took a second spaceflight in 1998 to test the abilities of an astronaut at the age of seventy-seven. Wouldn't it be a huge story if Wally gets to set a new record, and—as a woman—fly in space at an age a bit more than that? I'd love it!

Role models are important to all of us. I believe readers of this book will be inspired, as those who have known Wally personally have been, to do what they love, enjoy the people in their lives, and continue to pursue their goals despite potholes and speed bumps along the way.

EILEEN COLLINS
First Woman Space Shuttle Commander

Introduction

Some of the tests were painful. In one, the doctors inserted a large needle into the muscle at the base of my thumb. There was a wire coming out from the back of the needle, and they pulsed an electric current through it to test how well my nerves transmitted electrical signals. My nerves must have been working well because my hand clenched and opened, clenched and opened rapidly over and over. It hurt, and my forearm muscles got very tired. I was glad when they shut down the current and pulled the needle out.

I found out what barium tastes like. Drinking the thick, chalky liquid for a series of X-rays wasn't bad, though. Neither were the doses of castor oil or the pint of radioactive water I had to drink at other times that week. I found out, too, that barium is versatile. I had a barium enema for a different set of X-rays farther down my digestive tract. That was only one of half a dozen enemas I had to give myself in those five days.

I was X-rayed from head to toe, more than eighty images by my count. I had blood drawn, urine and stool samples taken, and EKG electrodes poked into my skin. I had to nudge the end of a three-foot-long rubber tube into my stomach by swallowing again and again. The doctors wanted to measure the acidity of my stomach fluids. I didn't care how painful or physically exhausting any of the tests were. I wanted to be an astronaut in the worst way.

I was in perfect health—something these and other

elaborate tests were designed to prove. It was 1961, and I was one of two dozen women who were taking the same rigorous physical exams the first American astronaut candidates had taken two years earlier at the Lovelace Clinic in Albuquerque, New Mexico. A handful of the men became famous as the Mercury 7, this country's first space travelers. We women who passed the physical exams became known as the Mercury 13. We never made it into space.

All of the first astronaut candidates were men. The selection criteria automatically excluded women, because women were not allowed to be military test pilots in those days. Dr. Randy Lovelace, whose Albuquerque clinic conducted the physical exams, wanted to see if women pilots could pass the same, painstaking tests. He thought female astronauts might offer some advantages over males.

Years later, Dr. Donald Kilgore, one of the supervising doctors, told a reporter, "We were told not to be easy on [the women], to give them the whole nine yards that the Mercury guys had gotten." He also said we complained less than the men had.

In fact, there were only two differences between our tests and the guys' tests. Anatomy caused one. A gynecological exam was added to the regimen for us. I had just turned twenty-two, and I learned what a pelvic exam entailed. The only stirrups I had used before were on horseback.

The other difference was logistical. The guys came to the clinic in groups of six, but the women came one or two at a time. The men had more chances to compete with one another and commiserate after the most unpleasant experiences. They also had more time to sit around and wait their turns for some of the tests. Their testing sessions lasted seven and a half days. I was there alone, and my tests were crowded into five days.

It turned out that NASA didn't want any women astronauts in those days. I didn't find that out until seven months later, when they abruptly canceled my next phase of testing. All through that long, tough physical exam and for months afterward, I believed I was on a path to actually become an astronaut. In one of the letters Dr. Lovelace had sent me, he wrote, "Examination of potential women astronauts is continuing." In a later letter, he wrote, "further tests have been arranged for the girls in the Woman-in-Space program who passed the initial examinations here at the Foundation." Jerrie Cobb, the first of us women to pass the physical exams, called the rest of us FLATS (Fellow Lady Astronaut Trainees). Why wouldn't I think I was really an astronaut candidate?

Then, suddenly, my dream of flying into space crashed hard to the ground. But I never gave up my dream of spaceflight. I held out for the future. I kept applying to NASA. I kept trying to better myself. I kept myself in top physical condition. I seized any opportunity I could to get more testing, to prove my capabilities as well as to learn about the challenges of space travel. After being turned down four times by NASA, I decided I would just have to find another way.

I never stopped pursuing spaceflight, but I didn't have blinders on. All of my adult life, I have been a passionate flying instructor, and I've had a wonderful career in aviation. I even broke a couple of glass ceilings for women along the way.

Let me tell you how it happened.

WALLY FUNK | *Spring 2020*

Chapter 1
The Fascination Begins

Supergirl

I was standing on the roof of the barn. Looking above the treetops toward the northeast, I saw the familiar glint of the morning sun on the huge rock slab near the top of Taos Mountain. I inhaled deeply, filling my lungs with the crisp, clean spring air. I was ready for my first attempt at flying.

The barn was a simple, wooden shed with a gently sloping roof. I had seen my father stretch his arms up to see if he could touch the edge of the roof there on the back side. He could almost do it. But at the age of five, I thought it was high enough to launch myself into flight.

Father wasn't there. He was at his store in town. Mother was in the kitchen planning the afternoon tea with her friends. I was wearing the Superman suit I had gotten for Christmas. I stretched out my arms, spreading the red cape as wide as I could. A gentle breeze carried the scent of the season's first lilac blossoms and fluttered the cape's edge. I was ready. I bent my knees, leaned forward, jumped, and flapped the cape with my arms.

Fortunately, I was realistic about my chances for immediate success and had piled loose hay on the ground to cushion my fall. I brushed brittle bits of the hay from my clothes, rearranged the pile, and climbed the ladder back up to the barn roof. Again, I spread my arms and waited for the breeze. This time, I thrust my legs harder as I leaped upward off the roof and flapped the cape as hard as I could. My only reward was hay stuck in my braids.

Why couldn't I fly? I knew I wasn't Superman; he was just a comic book character anyway. I had watched airplanes fly, though. My wings were broader than theirs, spreading from my hands to my back. Maybe it took more than wings to fly. Someday, I would find a way. Even now, decades later, I often think back to that day. In a way, it launched my lifelong adventure in aviation. The person I am today grew out of my childhood in the small northern New Mexico village of Taos. This was during the 1940s and early 1950s. Small towns were safe places then, and I learned to be independent. I learned that if I wanted to do something new, I had the ability to develop the skills I would need. I grew up feeling curious and capable of understanding.

I've been fascinated by machinery since I was old enough to walk. When I was two years old, Mother took a picture of me bending over to examine the nut on a tire of a DC-3 airplane parked at the Taos airport, to see how the wheel was attached to the strut. That was a special day at our little airport. The only airplane usually parked there was a Cessna 195 that belonged to a local photographer.

As I grew older, other girls my age were playing with dolls. Not me. I built a Lionel model train layout that snaked halfway through our house. My parents didn't seem to mind stepping over it as they went about their daily routines. One Christmas, I received an Erector Set and fashioned all sorts of railway bridges and towers out of its assorted beams, nuts, and bolts.

My first pre-flight safety inspection

    Model airplanes were my favorite things to build. There was something about flying that seemed magical to me. Father would bring me balsa wood kits from his Five and Ten Cent store. The kits came with patterns for the pieces each airplane would need. Sometimes I modified them based on visitors' airplanes I studied when I could talk Mother into driving me to the local airport to watch the activity. I had to draw and cut out each rib for the wings, the long stringers that made up the fuselage, and the small stringers that made up the elevator and the rudder. A razor blade worked best for cutting the splintery wood. I constructed the skeleton by gluing together all the parts. Then I was ready for the plane's skin. I pulled white tissue paper snugly over the rigid body and wings, dabbing dots of glue in strategic spots. To take the wrinkles out of the tissue paper and make it shrink skin tight, I sprayed a fine mist of water on it. When it dried, the paper was just as taut as the wing of a real airplane.

    One time, I couldn't find a spray bottle; so I went into Mother's room and picked up her perfume atomizer. I dumped the perfume in the sink and filled the bottle with water. It worked beautifully. When the paper dried, I brushed on base colors and designs using the little bottles of paint that we called "doping" in those days. I took my completed masterpiece to show Mother. As I described in detail how I had built it, I mentioned how I had used her perfume atomizer. Gently, she said, "Honey, I wish you had asked me first. We could have saved the perfume."

I didn't repeat that mistake, but I kept building model airplanes. I must have had twenty of them hanging by white thread from my bedroom ceiling by the time I was a teenager. Once, when I was talking with Mother about flying, she said, "Honey, you can always be a flight attendant."

I said, "No, I want to be in the front of the machine."

Sometimes, Father would take me along when he visited his other Five and Ten stores in Raton and Las Vegas (New Mexico) or on buying trips for merchandise. I was nine years old when we went on a buying trip to southern California. That's when I took my first airplane ride at the Santa Monica airport. It was in a two-engine Beech aircraft with my parents in the back and me in one of the two front seats. I had a great time looking at all the instruments and feeling the different forces acting on my body as we took off, made turns, came in, and landed. The pilot let me hold the yoke as he made turns. That was a big thrill.

Maybe it had something to do with my eventual love of flying, but I was always doing things on the roof. Mother would say, "Go up on the roof and put the luminarias up there." Luminarias are a traditional way of celebrating Christmas in New Mexico. You take a lunch-size, brown paper bag and put an inch or so of sand in the bottom. Then you press a votive candle down into the sand. When you have enough of them ready, you place them along the edge of the roof a foot or two apart. Then you go along and light each candle. The glowing bags are beautiful at night. I would put them up at Daddy's store, too.

Call Me "Wally"

Airplanes were an enduring interest, but I learned how to do other things, too. Some women carvers came to Taos when I was about ten years old, and I asked them to teach me how to make candlesticks. They showed me how to draw out a pattern for the diagonal lines I would carve into the rectangular block of wood. I would drill a hole in the top of the block for the candle and attach a base to the bottom of the block. Father bought me the tools I needed. I made many pairs of candlesticks, but I didn't treasure them like I did my model airplanes. I would take the candlesticks to Father's Five and Ten, set up a table in front of the store, and sell them to the tourists.

I sold lots of things in front of the store. I guess it was just in my nature to be productive. I grew squash, corn, and strawberries and sold them. I raised rabbits and sold them. I didn't care whether they were going to be pets or someone's dinner; either one would be useful. I made toy bows and arrows and sold them. I even set up a chair so I could shine the tourists' shoes. Once, Father asked me, "What are you doing with your money?"

I said, "I'm putting it in a jar."

He said, "That's good. Keep it there."

Mother told me about the spirit of Taos Mountain. She heard about it from the Taos Pueblo Indians. The mountain has always been sacred to the Indians, but even some Anglos could sense the spirit of the mountain. I was told some people will get the spirit of the mountain and some people won't. Later on, I found that when people come to see the famous mountain and they don't have the right frame of mind for it, they will never feel the desire to come back to Taos. But people who feel the spirit either stay or come back to stay. Mother knew about the spirit. She would say, "Open your drapes, clean your room, and look at the Taos Mountain for what you're supposed to do today." She didn't say "pray." She said, "Look at it, and it's going to tell you in your heart and in your mind what is expected of you to do today and what you're going to achieve." That's what I've done all my life.

I have lived and worked in many other places during my life, but Taos has always been my spiritual home. If I'm not there, I have a painting or a photograph of Taos Mountain on a wall in my home, and I look at that. I love that mountain. Its majestic form represents strength, stability, and endurance. Even now, when something happens that could be upsetting, I envision going to the clouds in Taos. I mentally go to the clouds and put whatever is bothering me in there, and I move on.

Since the turn of the twentieth century, a community of artists had been growing in Taos because of its historical blending of cultures and its inspirational landscape. Mother and Father were friends with many of the artists and entertained them often. Georgia O'Keeffe is probably the one most people today have heard of. Mable Dodge Luhan wasn't an artist, but she attracted a lot of famous people to visit or move to Taos. I got to know her as a child. I loved looking at the colorful ceiling in her dining room. The *latillas*, peeled tree branches placed at an angle and covering the ceiling between the beams, were painted red, black, and white to mimic the chevron patterns in Navajo weavings. My friends and I would sometimes play near her house or hide behind bushes and watch as elegantly dressed celebrities like Willa Cather, Aldous Huxley, Ansel Adams, Martha Graham, and

Lucille Ball came to Mrs. Luhan's extravagant parties.

The artists were active in the community. One of my favorite childhood memories was riding the antique carousel during the annual Taos fiesta. It had been restored by the Lions Club before I was born, and it was already old then. The date 1820 was stamped on the frame. The wooden horses were small and beautifully painted by some of the Taos artists, including Ernest Blumenschein, Oscar Berninghaus, and Rebecca Salsbury James. They were beautiful, bright colors—pink, purple, blue, orange, and even silver. We called the carousel *Tio Vivo* (Lively Uncle). It didn't have a motor. Two men turned a hand crank to make it go around. When they got tired, two other men would take their place. Father was a member of the Lions Club, and he always took his turn cranking the carousel. Two musicians played music while we were riding. When I was about eight years old, Universal Studios took the carousel to Hollywood for a while to use it in the movie *Ride the Pink Horse*. That was exciting for our little town.

Father had everything in his variety store—clothing and fabrics, candy, whatever anyone needed. The artists shopped there because he carried the particular paint brushes they preferred—the ones made out of squirrel fur. Artists would often come to our home for dinner parties. Mother was a gracious hostess. She had grown up in an elegant home in Olney, Illinois, where her father owned a bank. Her parents were invited to places like New York and Chicago because of their reputation, the way they acted, and what they did for people. There weren't the charities we have now, but Granddaddy always made sure that people were taken care of in Olney. He was tall and wore a top hat and a bow tie and beautiful clothes, and Nanna wore beautiful, long dresses. Mother was always dressed to the hilt. That's the way they lived.

My parents, Lozier and Virginia (Shy) Funk, were married in Illinois, but they moved to New Mexico in 1931. Father had tuberculosis, and his doctor advised him to move to a dry climate. They lived in Las Vegas, New Mexico, for several years before moving to Taos just before I was born. That's when Father opened the Five and Ten.

I saw my grandparents only on holidays. When they came to visit us in Taos, we went to the train station near Santa Fe and met them. They would stay a week and go back home. The house was absolutely spotless, and I was to be at the table at certain times and not speak unless spoken to. I remember my grandparents very vividly, but no conversations with them. I've been told that for my first Christmas, Mother was decorating a stocking for me, but my given name was too long to fit on it. So Granddaddy suggested shortening "Wallace," the middle name I had inherited from my great grandmother, to "Wally." It fit me better, too, and I've been Wally ever since.

Throw It a Fish

I always felt loved and cared for, but my parents also gave me a lot of freedom. When I would leave the house to ride my horse, Victor, or ride my bike, Mother would say, "If you fall and get hurt, brush yourself off and keep going. If you break a bone, come home, and we'll see the doctor."

I was given the great gift of confidence, and I've never had any fears. "No fears in our house," my parents would say. You have to understand how things work, and that way you can use them correctly and not have to be afraid of what might happen. Failure was not an option with my life; that's what my parents told me. Throughout my career and life, they encouraged me to meet whatever crisis came along with calm determination.

Victor and me in front of the barn where I played Superman

Sometimes Mother would ask me, "Where are you going to sleep tonight?" The answer might be in the barn, in the tree house I had built, outside under the stars, out with the Indians, or maybe even my bedroom.

I spent a lot of time with my Indian friends. A tribe of Indians has lived at Taos Pueblo since long before the first Europeans arrived in 1540.

I remember their summer fiestas, when the Indians would dress in colorful costumes, beat drums, and chant. Boys from the north side of the pueblo would run races against boys from the south side. Crowds of tourists and locals made it hard for me to see, but I would climb up on the roof of one of the adobe buildings or on one of the wooden frames they used for drying animal skins so I could see over the people and watch the races.

*The wooden racks in front are where
I'd climb to watch the races*

The Indians of Taos Pueblo were like a second family to me. They taught me how to fish and hunt and camp, and to survive in the wilderness. And they taught me a saying that I've used all my life. If something goes wrong and I can't do anything about it, I just say, "Throw it a fish" and let it go. I don't know how that expression came about. I imagine it might have referred to hungry animals pestering or threatening a person. If you throw it a fish, it will be satisfied and stop bothering you. Whatever its origin, that expression has always helped me deal with annoying or frustrating events. I enjoy my life, and I don't want to waste time and energy becoming upset or dwelling on issues I can't control. It's better to just let it go and move on.

An Indian couple worked for my parents. They came to our house by horse and wagon every day. Ben Romero took care of the yard, the animals, and exterior repairs. His wife, Christine, took care of the house and cooked dinner. I loved them both. I could get on the back of the wagon and swing my legs out while riding back to the pueblo with them. They lived on the south side of the pueblo, and I would go across the river, play with the horses, play in the river, and play with kids I knew.

Ben and Christine Romero with two deer Ben had hunted to feed their family.

I remember one of the times I went camping with some Indian friends. The trees weren't very high, but there was a lot of brush. The guys made a tent, but I wanted to sleep under the stars. They taught me how to make a fire by chipping with stones to make a spark. I had a great time that night. The stars were spectacular at 7,000 feet elevation with no light pollution.

Adventurous

I learned a lot from the artists and the Indians, but I learned from other people, too. One of them was Mrs. James, a dear family friend who was also my godmother. I often went to her house and helped her by picking eggs and herding pigs, and I learned how to milk cows. I learned how to drive a tractor for her when I was about ten. She had an old car that she let me drive starting when I was twelve or thirteen. I couldn't go very far because its radiator would run out of water. I'd go down to the creek, get water, and drive back to Mrs. James's. Father let me get my driver's license at fourteen. I knew about cars; I knew about machinery. I learned how to do that at Mrs. James's. I loved to go to her house because she had an outdoor john that I thought was fascinating. And she had a wood stove, which I loved because it was old.

Little cowgirl looking for a big adventure

I didn't read much, and I don't remember my parents reading to me when I was little. Father would bring me comic books from the Five and Ten. That's all I read. Some were good, historical comic books. I liked the cowboy ones, of course, being I was a little cowgirl. We didn't get a television set until I was fifteen. My parents were always happy for me when I found something new and different to do. I learned to tool leather and weave beaded bands. I competed in barrel racing in local rodeos. And I learned to shoot.

I got a BB gun when I was ten. When I was twelve, I got a .22 for Christmas from Mother's uncle. The next year, Taos High School started a junior rifle club, and I joined it. In the club's second year, I was the only girl on our five-person team. We were undefeated in New Mexico competitions. I really enjoyed target shooting. I remember I would walk from our house to the armory with my gun and my case with all my bullets and all the cleaning stuff every Wednesday. There were five different ratings, and I made them all. I completed the last one, Distinguished Rifleman, when I was barely sixteen.

At fourteen, I was on my way to becoming a Distinguished Rifleman.

I had to shoot at five-bull targets 50 feet away, in four different positions—lying prone, sitting, kneeling, and standing. All twenty of my shots were bullseyes. Mr. Bond, my instructor, sent the targets to the National Rifle Association in Washington, D.C., with my scores, and a letter came back from President Eisenhower, congratulating me.

In high school, I wanted to take classes in things I was interested in, like mechanical drawing and auto mechanics. But because I was a girl, I could only take home economics. I thought that was ridiculous, but I couldn't change their minds. Throw it a fish. I found other ways to learn the things I was interested in. I just have the mind to do something when people say it can't be done. I love challenges, and I like them hard. If I were growing up today, I'd want to be a Navy SEAL.

Skiing was another thing that I started early, probably around six years of age. At first, Daddy would pull me on a rope ten or twenty feet behind his car. He would drive slowly around the Taos plaza to help me learn to keep my balance on skis. Then I started skiing downhill at a small ski area called Sipapu southeast of Taos. I was fortunate to live near that ski area because it was the first one in New Mexico to install a ski lift. It was just a 100-foot tow rope, but I thought it was wonderful. Eventually, I competed in downhill, slalom, and ski jumping events. In 1955 I was on the team that represented New Mexico in the Western States American Legion junior ski championships in Sun Valley, Idaho.

I loved skiing, and I wanted to become good enough to compete in the Junior Olympics. During my junior year in high school, my parents arranged for me to spend half a semester training in Steamboat Springs, Colorado. I attended Steamboat Springs High School during that time, and I played drums in its famous ski band. It was a local tradition for the band to "march" on skis down Lincoln Avenue in the Winter Carnival parade in February. Our parade uniforms were what you would expect for a marching band: red pants with a white stripe; a white, double-breasted jacket with gold trim; and tall, white hats with a red band around them and a gold emblem on the front. But it snowed heavily during that year's Winter Carnival; so we just wore dark pants, white ski jackets, and winter hats with bills and ear flaps. We used short, cross-country skis, so "marching" straight down the street worked fine. But turning around while playing the bass drum was tricky. I could easily do a 180 on skis by doing a crisp kick turn, but to do it with that big drum strapped to my chest, I had to shuffle my skis around instead. Finding a way around challenges was always fun.

After I came back to Taos, Mother wrote to Stephens College in Columbia, Missouri, for information about its programs. It was a fashionable, two-year women's college where good students could finish high school while starting college. Some other girls from Taos had gone there. Later, a representative of Stephens came to Taos. He interviewed Father at his store, and then came to our home and talked to Mother. I'm not sure I made the right first impression when I came in from my outdoor activities wearing Levi's and a T-shirt, but I must have answered his questions well enough. He asked if I would like to go to Stephens. I didn't really know anything about it, but I said, "Sure." I agreed to enroll that fall. That's why I didn't graduate with my class at Taos High.

Not long after that, Father asked me to come upstairs to his office at the Five and Ten. He was working on his accounting books, and he said he wanted to teach me something. He showed me how to keep a record of everything I spent—how much it was and what it was for—and how to organize documents in folders. And he told me never to borrow or lend. I've always been grateful for what he taught me about operating a business, because I have been a business person all my life.

Father was the more businesslike of my parents. Mother was a very capable person, too, but she had grown up in more of a socialite family. As my sixteenth birthday approached, she wanted to arrange a coming out party for me in New York, like she had experienced. That was not my style. I could dress up nicely when I had to, but I was really a tomboy at heart. She didn't argue with me when I declined the offer. She always wanted the best for me, but she let me follow my own path.

In the fall of 1956, my parents drove me to the railroad station in Lamy, eighteen miles south of Santa Fe, and I boarded the train for my first year of college in Missouri.

Wally Funk

That was the beginning of an entirely new kind of learning experience.

CHAPTER 2
I Sprout Wings

STEPHENS COLLEGE

The drive from Taos to the train station in Lamy, near Santa Fe, took over two hours. I had everything I would need at Stephens College packed in an overnight bag, two matching suitcases, and a trunk. They were stashed in the back of our Ford station wagon, the kind that had wooden panels on the sides. The letter the admissions office had sent me listed certain things that were necessary to bring. It was going to be a "hats-hose-heels-gloves" type of atmosphere. We could wear only dresses to classes, and we had to dress properly for dinner each evening.

Stephens arranged for trains with sleeping cars and dining cars to gather its students from the western states. Everyone on the train was going to the same place. All the girls there were well dressed and had their nails done. They were smoking cigarettes in those long holders that were fashionable in the mid-1950s. My father smoked Camel cigarettes, and I hated the smell. Now here were all these girls trying to be elegant by smoking. "What have I gotten myself into?" I thought.

Mother had made sure I was dressed nicely for the trip.

*My "hat-hose-heels-gloves"
ensemble for the train*

When I got on the train on September 10, 1956, I was wearing a white blouse with dark lace trim on the collar, a short jacket, a flared dark skirt with black trim, a beret that matched the skirt's trim, and black pumps with one-inch heels. At 5 feet 8 inches, I didn't need to add much height. I started to meet my classmates. By the time the train pulled out of New Mexico, there were twenty-two other girls from the state aboard. I was the only one from Taos.

I was on the train from Monday morning until Tuesday afternoon. On Monday evening about seven o'clock, I penned a postcard to my parents. "Didn't think I would be writing so soon, but there's nothing to do, but sing and cut up," I wrote. I told them the roast duckling I had for dinner wasn't bad. I also mentioned that I couldn't go to dinner in my Bermuda shorts; so I put a skirt on over them. Obviously, I had dressed down to be more comfortable after boarding the train.

When we arrived in Columbia, Missouri, we stepped off the train and searched through the mounds of luggage for our own pieces. We took taxies to campus or got rides from some friendly young men who offered to drive us. The campus was lovely, with stately trees and white-trimmed, red brick buildings.

I had almost enough credits to finish high school, and I could finish those at Stephens. So I skipped my senior year at Taos High. Stephens was a two-year college, and they classified their first-year students as juniors and their second-year students as seniors.

We first-year students attended a welcoming assembly, had a tour of the library, and were treated to a picnic where we were allowed to wear knee-length shorts. Then we took a series of tests to identify our interests and aptitudes. Along with academic courses like English, history, and foreign languages, Stephens offered vocational courses like fashion design, retailing, television and radio, and business. I decided to major in physical education. I spent a lot of time in the gym that semester. I felt at home there, and I didn't have to wear a dress.

It didn't take long to settle into the student routine. On Sundays, all students were expected to attend the nondenominational service on campus or the service at a church of their choice in town. One service at the beginning of the year was the traditional White Sunday, when we had to wear the all-white dresses and accessories we had been instructed to bring. There would be another White Sunday at the end of the school year.

We wore mid-calf dresses or skirts and blouses to classes. Many of the skirts were full, and even the "straight" skirts had a slight flare. This was a time and place for modesty and decorum. Our feet sported loafers or black-and-white saddle oxfords with bobby socks, or flat or low-heeled pumps with nylon stockings. I could only wear my favorite outfit, Levi's and a T-shirt, in the dorm.

Let's Try Something Else

I felt out of place at first. But the other girls were friendly, and in a few days, I started to fit in. There were fun things to do besides going to classes. For instance, even though fashion wasn't one of my main interests, I was one of half a dozen girls who were written up in the local paper sporting our raccoon coats during football season.

Wearing the latest fashion fad is part of the fun of being in college

I joined the school's symphony orchestra. Music had been important to me back in Taos. When I was about ten or twelve, I would put the old 78 records on the folks' big record player in the dining room, where the long, handmade wooden table was. I'd put the opera on because I loved it so much, and Mother listened to it a lot. I would get out pots and pans of different sizes, turn them upside down on the tablecloth, and play them with wooden spoons along with the recording. Or I would conduct the orchestra with a wooden utensil. Mother walked in on me one time when I was doing it, and she got a kick out of it and took my picture. Sometimes the folks would tell me to choose an opera record and give them a little show before dinner. I was serious about it because at that time, I wanted to be an orchestra conductor. When I was older, they took me to the Santa Fe Opera. The performances in its lovely outdoor setting were, and still are, nationally acclaimed.

I had started playing a clarinet in my school band in Taos. After I was on that for a while, Mother said, "You know, honey, I don't want your teeth to get pushed out; so try something else." So I started learning how to play the trumpet, and she said, "You know, you're pushing up against your teeth." They were so careful because they knew I was going to have to have braces. "Let's try something else," she said, and then I got on percussion.

I played percussion in the orchestra at Stephens, and sometimes we played for opera productions. In November of my first year there, a few members of our orchestra, including me, were invited to play with the St. Louis Symphony Orchestra. Playing percussion with that professional orchestra was a thrill.

My roommate was Sidney Bass. I really surprised her one day. I'd been out for a walk, thinking about how I missed all the animals back home, and I found a frog in a pond. I brought it back to my room and put it on the rim of the bathtub. When Sidney saw it, it scared her to death. I was just horsing around. I've always been a playful, happy person. She said, "I can't go take a bath with that frog on there."

I said, "It's not going to hurt you." She was from Florida after all. She must have seen frogs there.

In December, I took the train to Kansas City and flew TWA home for the holidays. What a joy it was to be back in Taos! One of the first things I wanted to do was go skiing. Taos Ski Valley had opened the year before in the mountains north of town. It had only one run then, with a simple tow rope that skiers could grab onto and be pulled about 200 feet up the mountain. I belonged to the ski patrol there, and when I came back, I started enjoying their new, longer trail known as Al's Run. They had installed a second-hand Poma lift on it. It had little round platforms attached to rods that hung down from a moving cable. As one of the seats moved past, a skier would straddle the rod and rest their bottom on the platform while being pulled up the slope. It could take skiers almost 1,000 vertical feet up the mountain. That was as high as any lift in New Mexico then.

The Poma lift ran about twice as fast as most T-bar lifts do; so it was fun to ride. On one of my trips up, as I got up to about the third tower of the lift, the cable suddenly derailed and flipped me about 20 feet into the air. The snow cushioned my fall a little, but I still landed hard. The snow was at least 6 feet deep, and I sank down into it. It was so deep people had a hard time finding me, even though I was yelling out at them. It seemed like I waited a long time for them to find me. I've always been a happy person; so I was smiling and joking while they carried me down and put me in a car. I was sitting up while they drove me to my house, but I probably should have been lying down. When we got home, Mother took me to the emergency room. They found a couple of cracked vertebrae; so they fitted me with a half-body brace that I had to wear until my back healed.

Taking Flight

I spent the first several days back at Stephens standing up in the back of my classrooms because it was uncomfortable to sit for an hour in the brace. I didn't mind wearing it for half of the semester. But I was a physical education major, and I couldn't participate in physical activities. My grades started to go down. After a few weeks, Dr. Bates, my advisor, called Mother. He said, "Mrs. Funk, your daughter's not doing very well in her classes."

Mother said, "Do you have an airport out there?"

"Yes."

"Get her out there, and set her flying," she said.

Mother understood my passion for airplanes. In fact, I think I inherited it from her. She first took a ride in a bi-wing airplane in Olney, Illinois, when she was sixteen. A barnstormer landed in a field near her school. She ran out of the schoolroom and told the pilot, "I want a ride."

He said, "I need a dollar a minute."

So she went back to her friends and borrowed a dollar from each one. She came back to the pilot and said, "I have ten dollars."

"Get in."

She told me the first thing they did was a loop, and she loved it. Then they did a roll and some turns. That evening, she told her daddy, "I want to fly."

"Absolutely not!" he said. "You are a young lady. You will learn to be a good wife and a good mother. That is your role in life."

Remember, that was the 1920s, when Amelia Earhart and Bobbi Trout were setting aviation records. He thought it was undignified that women pilots wore britches. Mother didn't tell me that story until maybe twenty years after I got my licenses, but when she did, I finally understood why she told Dr. Bates to get me to an airport when I was seventeen.

I had a great opportunity at Stephens because during World War II, when women had to take over many traditionally male jobs, the college had added an aviation course of study to its curriculum. As soon as I changed my major to aviation, I felt more like I was where I belonged.

For one thing, the dress code allowed aviation students and horseback riders to wear pants on days they had those classes. I managed to schedule my aviation classes five days a week.

The biggest benefit was learning to fly, though. I took aeronautics classes and flying lessons. My flying instructor, Tower Creasy, taught very gently. He never used harsh language or raised his voice. I learn by the seat of my pants. He showed me; then I responded. And that's how I learned to fly. It wasn't really out of reading a book; it was show and tell. Later, when I learned to fly acrobatics, I would look at the picture, have somebody show me, and off I'd go.

At 8:45 the morning of Thursday, December 5, 1957, I wrote a postcard to my parents from the Columbia Municipal Airport. I was too excited to be careful about spelling and punctuation as I wrote, "Hi. I *'soloed'* this am at 7:30 AM. I'm so excited I don't know what to do. Am on my way now to a aviation test, that I'm going to pass with flying colors. Wally." I passed that written test, too, and got my private pilot's license. I soloed in a great airplane, a 1947 Cessna 120. Besides having my license, I had to complete 100 miles of flying to graduate from Stephens. I would fly around the countryside, and once I even flew up to Olney, Illinois, where my mother was visiting. I flew her as my first passenger. I think she was as thrilled as I was.

Stephens' Aviation Club was open to anyone interested in air transportation. Those of us who were pilots participated in its Flight Team and competed at National Intercollegiate Flying Association (NIFA) air meets each year. There were two dozen of us, and we were known as the Flying Susies. All the students at Stephens were called Susies. Our flight team competed nationally with both junior and senior colleges. In May 1958, I was the only Flying Susie to win a trophy at the

NIFA meet at Macalester College in St. Paul, Minnesota. The Oklahoma State Flying Aggies won the team competition that year, as they had for the previous three years.

Now I knew where I wanted to go after I graduated from Stephens. It wasn't an easy decision, though. I loved music and still dreamed of becoming an orchestra conductor. I loved flying, too. I had been able to do both of those at Stephens, but now I had to decide on a career path. Flying won out because it was so exciting. It was more active than sitting and reading notes. There's more to do—takeoffs and landings, and keeping an eye on the instrument displays. And it was working with a piece of mechanical equipment, like the cars and tractors I had worked on back in Taos. I applied for admission to Oklahoma State University.

Right after Stephens' graduation in May, Father drove me to Stillwater, Oklahoma, and I started summer school at Oklahoma State. After I'd started flying, I didn't have trouble with my grades anymore. That summer I earned a B in American Government and an A in Intermediate Flight. I was majoring in education, but my main interest was being a Flying Aggie. By the time the fall semester began, I felt at home on campus.

Mother wanted me to join a sorority; so I became an Alpha Chi Omega. It was all right, but I wasn't really the sorority girl type. We would have formal dances, and I would get dressed up and say my hellos to people there. Then I would go back to my room, change my clothes, climb out the window, and go flying.

FLYING IS FREEDOM

That November, I joined the Oklahoma Chapter of the Ninety-Nines. The Ninety-Nines is an international organization of women pilots. Amelia Earhart was elected its first president in 1931, and its name came from the fact that there were ninety-nine charter members. Now that I had my private pilot's license, I was eligible to join. The girls I met there seemed like sisters to me.

Of course, I joined the Flying Aggies Club at the start of the fall semester. There were over sixty members that semester, and about a dozen were girls. We had a great time having wiener roasts at the Stillwater airport and flying to different places around the state for breakfast events or to see football games. Parties at Halloween and Christmas were casual and fun. And, of course, there were lots of practice air meets to sharpen our skills for outside competitions.

I was lucky again in having great instructors, especially Tiner Lapsley. He was the head of the program and a kind, gentle teacher. I stepped right into the program because I had such great preparation at Stephens. In late October, we faced the Oklahoma University Air Knockers in our first meet of the season. The Flying Aggies took the team trophy, and I finished first in the power-off landing event, touching down at a certain point on the runway with the engine just idling instead of controlling the speed during the landing.

Instruction for the Flying Aggies was special. In most programs, an instructor flew with one student at a time. But in the Oklahoma State program, three of us would go with one instructor on a 1,000-mile cross-country flight. One student would be at the controls of the airplane while the other two were practicing and getting advice on navigating and radio communications. It was like getting three times the flying time for the same cost, because we only had to pay for the time we were actually at the controls. We had another financial perk, too. The public paid $8 an hour for flying time, but we only had to pay $5 an hour.

I hung out at the airport, gassing up airplanes and helping the mechanics. I even volunteered to mow the grass between the runways in exchange for flying time. They had a single-engine seaplane—a Piper Cub the Oklahoma State mechanics had put pontoons on—that we learned to fly at Lake Carl Blackwell eight miles west of town or at Boomer Lake in town.

My OSU instructor Tiner Lapsley and me with the Piper Cub seaplane.

I joined the Stillwater Soaring Society and soloed on my fifth glider flight. Flying a glider was really fun. We used a two-seater Laister-Kauffman sailplane made in Germany. An airplane would take off, towing the glider on a long rope. The glider would become airborne before the airplane did because it was lighter and more aerodynamically efficient. After being released from the airplane, I would fly maneuvers in the glider and enjoy soaring in silence. Once, I flew really high. I was soaring with the birds, thinking about how I'd loved watching them fly back home in Taos.

When I landed, the guys said, "How come you were up there so long?"

I said, "Because I caught an updraft and went up to 14,000 feet and circled there for a while."

"You're a girl. You can't get up that high," they said.

"You look at the barograph," I said. And they ate their words.

It was good-natured kidding, though. I got along well with the guys on the team. We were interested in the same things, and we all loved flying. In my senior year, the Flying Aggies decided to host a breakfast fly-in. We thought it would be a good way to connect Stillwater with other flying enthusiasts around the state. We expected about 200 people to show up, which we could just about handle with our $50 budget. When the morning of Sunday, March 27, 1960, arrived, it seemed like the airplanes would never stop coming in. At final count, the turnout was 226 aircraft and 521 people. We had to scramble for support from a couple of local folks who donated more food.

There were several other girls in the Flying Aggies, but I was the only one that qualified to compete in the NIFA air meets my two years at Oklahoma State. About fifty of us would compete in a dozen practice meets in the months leading up to the national meet, and the top fifteen would go on to the national meet. Along with our sponsors and ground crew members, we flew to the NIFA meets in eight small planes. Those national meets in May were the most challenging and the most fun. Twenty-five or thirty schools would send teams from all over the country.

The Flying Aggies expanded the informal activities to include "bronc riding."

How hard could a fake horse be for a real cowgirl?

Of course, we wore our competition uniforms for this event too: dressy white coveralls, black cowboy hats, and western boots with decorative stitching. We brought along four wood posts, ropes, a 55-gallon drum, and a saddle. With the poles planted in the ground, we would tie ropes between the barrel and each of the posts, put the saddle on the barrel, and invite competitors to ride it while we pulled and jerked on the ropes. We always managed to buck them off. Once, I told the guys, "You try to buck me off." They couldn't. But then, maybe they didn't try hard enough. We had our team pride, after all.

The official NIFA competition includes lots of questions and answers, tests, and preflight checks for your airplane. The precision flying events were the most exciting, though. The national air meet was held in Champaign, Illinois, my junior year and in Columbus, Ohio, my senior year. There were four flying events, each with a team score and individual scores.

The landing event actually had two versions, power on and power off. The idea was to land with your main gear touching down right on a marked line on the runway. Similarly, there were two types of takeoff events, soft field and short field. Soft field techniques would be used for a grass runway or a hard runway that was covered with snow or slush, for example. And for the short-field takeoff, you would have to clear an obstacle 50 feet down the runway.

The cross-country navigation event could be particularly tricky. You had to find certain checkpoints in a sequence. For example, you might fly on a certain heading until you flew over a farm house of a particular color, then change to a different heading and fly about 100 miles until you found where a railroad crossed a highway. After completing several checkpoints, you would arrive back at the airport, and your score was based on the time you took to complete the course.

My favorite event was the bomb drop. We didn't actually drop bombs, of course. We used a five-pound sack of flour. There would be a round target painted on the grass somewhere. When it was your turn, you flew over it and dropped the bomb so it would land in there. You had to know the winds and how fast the airplane was going. One of my teammates would fly a Cessna 150, and I would open the door and climb halfway out. My leg was hanging on in the cockpit and I was hanging onto the wing as we approached the target that was a hundred feet below us. As we got close to the target, I would tell the pilot to slow the airplane down, and then I would whomp the sack down. I got it in the circle every time. That was great!

The two years I competed with the Flying Aggies, we continued our dominance in NIFA air meets. In both 1959 and 1960, we won the team competition. And both years I came away with trophies for the Flying Aggie Top Pilot and the Ninety-Nines Achievement Award. The Ninety-Nines trophy recognized the outstanding Ninety-Nines member competing in the meet, and it was a great honor.

Higher Faster Longer

By the time I graduated from Oklahoma State in 1960, I had earned my commercial, single-engine land, multi-engine land, single-engine sea, glider, instrument, flight instructor, and all ground instructor ratings. I was ready to fly for a living.

Pat Conner had been my roommate at Oklahoma State. Her father was an officer at Fort Sill, near Lawton, Oklahoma. Pat and I decided to go there and have a good time that summer before looking for jobs. We drove down and got all our stuff unpacked. That evening, Pat's father said, "What are you two girls going to do?"

Pat said, "We're just going to play."

He was very stern. He said, "Pat, you're going to go out to the stables, and you're going to work with the horses. Wally, you're going to go out to the airport and fly."

We did exactly that. The next day, Pat got a job, and I got a job. I went over to the airport and started asking around. I met a man who was a member of Fort Sill's Red Leg Flying Club, and I said, "Do you need a flight instructor?"

He said, "Yes. When can you start?"

I said, "Tomorrow. I need a uniform." All the ratings I had earned and the trophies I had won showed I was competent. I went to work as an instructor for the Army, where I taught noncommissioned and commissioned officers to fly. I was the first civilian flight instructor hired at Fort Sill. I earned $4.00 an hour. I racked up flying hours, and I got more specialized training myself. I enjoyed working there. The military regimen felt natural to me.

I stayed with the Conners for a while, and sometimes Pat's father would come home and tell me he heard a comment about what a good job I was doing. Knowing that he was proud of what I was doing was a great inspiration for me.

It was wonderful to know that I could earn a living

flying. Flying is freedom. I actually feel like I am closer to God when I am high in the sky. There is so much you can do up there in the air. There's nothing else that compares with soaring above the Earth, able to move easily in any direction. I had no idea that I would soon discover an even more exhilarating possibility.

Chapter 3
I Want Some Space

Potential Lady Orbiter

It was late October 1960, and I was taking a break in the flying club at Fort Sill. The place smelled like coffee that had been kept hot too long, but I didn't care. I was drinking water. Mother always told me water was the best thing to drink. I picked up the new issue of *Life* magazine. The cover image was actress Nancy Kwan, star of the new movie *Suzie Wong*. I didn't really care about that, but you never knew what interesting topics the magazine might have inside. I was flipping through the pages when I saw a black-and-white photo of a woman floating on her back in a tank of water. That seemed unusual, but what really caught my eye was the headline: "Damp Prelude to Space." Under that, a smaller headline said, "A potential lady orbiter excels in lonesome test."

Space was on everyone's mind those days. Back in 1957, the Soviet Union had put the first satellite in Earth orbit, and a month later sent a living dog into orbit. Two months ago, in August 1960, two Russian dogs had landed safely after orbiting the Earth seventeen times. It wouldn't be long before people went into space. It had been a year and a half since NASA named America's first space travelers—seven men who were now training to be astronauts. Last March, the Soviets announced their first group of space men. They called them cosmonauts. And here in this magazine, a *woman* was being tested to become an astronaut.

It wasn't just any woman, either. It was someone I knew. Jerrie Cobb was a renowned, record-setting pilot who, like me, worked in Oklahoma and was also a member of the Ninety-Nines. Wow, I wanted in on this action! I figured if Jerrie could do it, I could do it. The article was about a "sensory deprivation" test she had taken, and it described the reasoning behind it this way:

To a person alone in orbit, weightless and sealed in, the lack of sensory stimuli can be a grave danger. This is because the human brain, when it receives no messages from the outside, no jolts of electricity from the nerve ends of the body, is apt to lapse into an irresponsible state of dreaminess and even of hallucination. To a space traveler who may have to react in split seconds after dreary hours of doing nothing, the ability to remain in touch with reality is all important.

Space travel was going to be uncharted territory, and I wanted to be part of it. I didn't waste any time. That same day, I wrote to Jerrie and to Dr. Jay T. Shurley, the psychiatrist the magazine identified as the person who designed and administered the test to Jerrie at the VA hospital in Oklahoma City.

In just a few days, I received a letter from Dr. Shurley. He explained that the test he had given Jerrie was not officially part of the potential astronaut examination program that was being administered by Dr. W. Randolph Lovelace II. He was kind enough to include the mailing address for Dr. Lovelace in Albuquerque, New Mexico. Back in early

1959, Dr. Lovelace had been in charge of developing and administering the physical exams for NASA's Mercury astronaut candidates. They were military test pilots, which meant that they were all men. Women did not have a chance to become military pilots in those days. After testing the guys, Dr. Lovelace wondered if women could be fit enough to be astronauts. If so, they could save NASA money on each launch because women generally weigh less than men and use less food and oxygen. And some tests indicated women might be a better fit psychologically, too. Dr. Lovelace had tested Jerrie first, and she did so well that he wanted to test other women pilots, too.

Right away, I was back at my typewriter, pecking out a letter to Dr. Lovelace. "I am most interested in these tests to become an astronaut," I wrote. "This has been ever since I started to fly." I included a list of my aviation licenses and ratings, adding that I had logged over 600 hours of flying and gliding time and was currently working as a civilian flight instructor teaching military personnel at Fort Sill.

Things moved quickly. On November 11, just six days after I typed my letter to Dr. Lovelace, he dictated a response. His letter came with a card listing the background information I had to provide. It included aviation experience, basic health information, education credentials, and even some personal things like church affiliation. I filled it out and asked a couple of people to write letters of recommendation for me.

After the whirlwind of the application process, things seemed to grind to a sluggish pace. I waited for a response from Dr. Lovelace. It didn't come until the first week of February 1961, but it was worth waiting for. The key sentence jumped off the page: "We have reviewed the credentials you have sent in and find that you are acceptable for these examinations." Yes! The letter went on to say that the room and board expenses for the women's tests were being provided by Jackie Cochran, a prominent woman pilot who had organized the WASP program during World War II. While the men pilots were flying in combat, members of the Women's Airforce Service Pilots (WASPs) were trained to deliver planes to overseas bases, tow targets through the air for gunnery training in this country, and serve as flight instructors for military pilots. Jackie had drawn national attention to the abilities of women pilots.

Lovelace's letter also said that the program would be kept confidential until all the participants had been tested. The other important information was the date of my exam. I was to arrive in Albuquerque on Sunday, February 26, 1961, and report to the Lovelace Clinic the following morning at eight o'clock without eating, drinking, chewing gum, or smoking (which I didn't do anyway) after midnight. My week of testing would end the following Saturday by noon.

This was not going to be like any medical exam I had ever taken. The women's qualifications were similar to the men's: no more than thirty-five years old, no more than 5 feet 11 inches tall, qualified pilots with substantial experience in the air, with FAA commercial pilot certification and instrument rating. I've always been athletic, and I didn't drink or smoke. And now I was working to get into the best possible shape. I rode my bicycle to work every day at Fort Sill, about eight miles round trip. I did 100 sit-ups and 20 push-ups every day. As my exam date got closer, I went home to Taos and got in some high-altitude exercise.

Lovelace Clinic

On the appointed day, my parents drove me to Albuquerque, and I checked into the Bird of Paradise motel across the street from the Lovelace Clinic. The motel was a little shabby, but I didn't care. I was only going to be sleeping there, after all. I was the youngest of the female candidates, having just turned twenty-two. The age range for candidates was twenty-five to thirty-five, but my qualifications were so strong they made an exception for me. Still, Mother and Father had to sign a permission form to allow me to participate. Someone from the clinic came to the motel with the permission form and a list of the coming week's activities.

I looked over the three-page schedule that outlined each of the five days of testing. The first three days started with no mention of breakfast. That improved a little on Thursday, when the schedule said, "Upon completion of X-rays you may eat breakfast if time permits." Finally on Friday, I could look forward to a real breakfast, with my first appointment not until 8:30. I saw that lunch was on the schedule every day, although on one day it was to be "a light lunch, prior to exercise tests." The other things they gave me were two containers, one marked "urine" and one marked "stool."

At seven o'clock Monday morning, I reported to the laboratory appointment desk and turned in my urine cup. I was pleasantly surprised to find that after the lab samples were drawn, I had time for a quick breakfast before I reported to my eight o'clock appointment. That first physical evaluation was the first of what turned out to be many times during the week that I would be hooked up for an electrocardiogram. The Master's Two-Step test consisted of stepping up and down two 12-inch steps in time with a metronome. That was easy for me. Growing up being active in sports in the high altitude around Taos had been good conditioning.

The next test was easy, too, just a hearing exam and an evaluation of my ability to speak clearly. I guess they wanted to make sure astronauts could communicate well with the people on the ground during their flight. I had to read a special paragraph that contained all the common sounds of the English language:

You wish to know all about my grandfather. Well, he is nearly ninety-three years old; he dresses himself in an ancient black frock coat, usually minus several buttons; yet he still thinks as swiftly as ever. A long, flowing beard clings to his chin, giving those who observe him a pronounced feeling of the utmost respect. When he speaks his voice is just a bit cracked and quivers a trifle. Twice each day he plays skillfully and with zest upon our small organ. Except in the winter when the ooze of snow or ice prevents, he slowly takes a short walk in the open air each day. We have often urged him to walk more and smoke less, but he always answers, "Banana oil!" Grandfather likes to be modern in his language.

The ten o'clock test was less comfortable. It was called the cold pressor test. I had to hold my hand in water that had ice floating in it for as long as I could, and they kept measuring my blood pressure and heart rate. Then I did it with my other hand and each of my feet. After getting some instructions for the afternoon tests, I took a break for lunch.

Then it was time to follow the instructions I had gotten that morning. I had never had an enema before, much less given myself one, but I did what I had been told and got through the embarrassing rectal exam. After that, I had my sinuses X-rayed. Next came the pulmonary function tests where they measured my lung capacity by having me take as deep a breath as I could and then blow into a mask to empty my lungs. After ten hours, my first day of testing ended.

The guys who had taken these tests for NASA came in groups of six; so they had other people to share the experience and compete with. The women came two at a time, but the gal who was there the same time I was left after a few hours. I don't know what the reason was, but I was there doing the tests alone that week. I didn't meet any of the other women, although I knew Jerrie Cobb from before.

When I reported to the laboratory at 7:30 Tuesday morning, the nurse wanted to talk to me about those two cups I had been given on Sunday evening. I had turned in the one marked "urine" Monday morning. But now, the nurse said, "Wally, you haven't given us the other cup."

I said, "I don't know what 'stool' means. The only thing 'stool' means to me is when I was sitting on a stool milking cows in Taos." I had no idea.

She said, "No, that's when you poo."

I said, "You don't want that, do you?"

"Yes, we want that. We can tell a lot about your body from that."

Okay. If they wanted some of my poo, I'd give it to them. I didn't care how strange any of their requests or procedures might be; I'd go right along with them.

One test that day was pretty ordinary. I just had to walk on a treadmill.

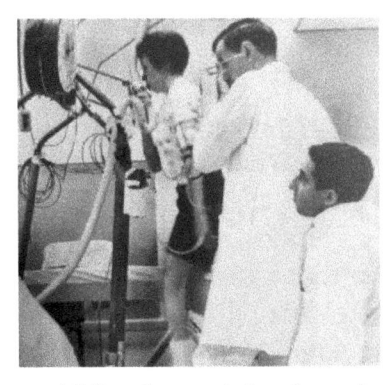

My outdoorsy childhood comes in handy on the treadmill.

My nose was clamped shut, and a breathing apparatus filled my mouth. I was also hooked up to a blood pressure cuff. I didn't have to walk too fast, just two miles an hour, and for only three minutes.

Another test felt a little awkward. I had to undress and sit naked in a chair that was then lowered completely into a large tank of water after I had expelled the air from my lungs. The chair was attached to a scale so they could record my weight while I was under water. I don't know how guys feel about being naked in front of other people, but it certainly wasn't something I was used to. But being an astronaut was more important to me than being uncomfortable, whether it was physically or emotionally. I had made up my mind to do whatever I had to do to pass those tests. This particular test let the doctors measure the specific gravity of my body. Later I found out this could give them an idea of the relative amounts of muscle, bone, and fat in my body.

Other tests were even stranger. I had to drink a cup of radioactive water and give urine samples every half hour all morning. Then they injected dye into my blood stream and wanted more urine samples. They X-rayed my back and every tooth in my mouth. The day ended with something called a gastric analysis test. They ran a three-foot section of rubber hose down my throat so they could get a sample of what was in my stomach.

Back at the motel that evening, I wrote a postcard to my parents: "Hi. I'm still making it, although they have me on a liquid diet and [I'm] very weak in the physical part. I beat Jerry [sic] Cobb's average on one test which I'm real happy about. I found out that joking and just being me has helped no matter how much the pain and being uncomfortable it is. I guess if you want something bad enough you can withstand about anything. Think I know every Dr. & nurse here. Just had a gastric test—I'll never be the same. Love, Wally."

You're Better Than That

Yes, some of the tests were painful, but I remembered Mother's advice from when I was a kid. She would say, "See that baby crying over there because it didn't get its way or it bumped its elbow? You don't do that. You're better than that." Some of the tests may have hurt, but I didn't let it get me down. I wanted so badly to go into space that the pain didn't matter to me.

Wednesday was another full day. I wasn't sure what barium was, but we used a lot of it during the tests. Sometimes we drank it, and sometimes we used it in an enema. I forget which it was that day, but it got me ready for many more X-rays. By the time the week was over, I think I counted about 85 X-rays.

The most exhausting task of the week was the stationary bicycle test. I had a blood pressure cuff on my arm and wires stuck into my skin at various places to keep track of my pulse rate and I don't know what all. My nose was clamped shut, and I had a breathing device in my mouth so the doctors could measure my oxygen consumption. They told me to pedal with the beat of a metronome, and I started riding. It was easy at first, but they gradually added resistance on the rear tire to make it feel like I was riding up an increasingly steep hill. I was supposed to ride until I was completely exhausted. They said that usually took ten minutes; so of course I challenged myself to pedal longer than that. I got to about seven minutes, and I pulled out my second wind. I went and I went. Sweat was stinging my eyes and dripping off my chin. At about nine and a half minutes I thought, "Okay, I don't know if it's there, but I need my third wind."

I pushed all my blood up into my upper body, and I got my mind settled for a third wind. I got it, and I went to eleven minutes.

When I stopped, I was more tired than I had ever been in my life. They offered to help me off the bike, but I said, "No, I can get off myself, but can you take these needles out of my body first?" After they removed the wires, I stepped off the bike, and I fell flat on the floor. My legs had no strength left, but I was happy that I had made it to eleven minutes.

Thursday started with an eye exam that lasted a few hours. They tested my normal vision, night vision, recovery from darkness, depth perception, and ability to focus on a moving object. They measured the pressure inside my eyeballs and photographed the inside of each eyeball. There were seventeen different tests. As a pilot, I'd had eye exams before, but this was way beyond that.

Next, I boarded an airplane for a flight to Los Alamos National Laboratory in northern New Mexico. The birthplace of the atomic bomb, the Lab still did a lot of research with radiation, and I was told I would be examined to determine my total body radiation. I didn't even know I had any. During the flight, I wrote another postcard to my parents. One side had a photograph of Leonard's Fine Foods, a restaurant on Albuquerque's Central Avenue. I wrote, "Hi—had a good lunch here yesterday after a 24 hr. diet of liquid. Ate at the Alvarado last nite. Think I passed a very extensive eye test today—have a vertigo test with the ears today also. We are flying to Los Alamos. … Am getting almost worn out but must keep going. Love to all—Wally." The Alvarado was a beautiful, historic hotel and restaurant at the railroad station in Albuquerque, part of the famous Harvey House chain. Finally, I was getting to enjoy some tasty meals!

The landing approach to the Los Alamos airport made

me feel like I was going home. Like Taos, it had an elevation of about 7,000 feet. Ahead, I could see beautiful northern New Mexico mountains—not my beloved Taos Mountain, but beautiful anyway. After landing, we drove to Los Alamos National Laboratory, and I was taken to a basement room with a big, green metal cylinder lying on its side. There was an adjoining dressing room, where I had to scrub my body down to fresh skin. I put on a white pajama-like outfit and paper slippers. Back in the larger room, I climbed a few steps and lay down in a drawer that extended out of the thick cylinder.

They slid the drawer into the cylinder, and it closed with a heavy, metallic clunk. I was in a very small space. My arms were crossed over my chest, and the inside of the tube was only about 8 inches above my face. I guess it may have made some people feel claustrophobic, because they showed me where a "chicken switch" was in case I panicked and needed to come out quickly. But the close quarters didn't bother me. It was hard to judge time, but after five or ten minutes, they pulled the drawer out again. The test was over. Back to the airplane and Albuquerque for what turned out to be the most painful test of all.

When I got back to the Lovelace Clinic, a nurse took me to a room and told me to sit down in what looked like a dentist's chair. The nurse strapped my arms to the armrests and tilted the chair back a little. The doctor said, "We're going to inject water in your ears."

I said, "Okay."

They used a large syringe and injected a stream of water into my ear for 30 seconds. The water turned out to be really cold. I was told it was 10 degrees Centigrade, or 50 degrees Fahrenheit. That doesn't sound very cold, but it felt like ice water. After all, it was almost 50 degrees colder than my normal body temperature. Like everyone, I had sometimes poked into my ear too far while cleaning it, and I knew how that hurt. This hurt a lot more. It numbed my inner ear and disrupted my sense of balance. It was a good thing I was strapped in that chair. The disturbing dizziness lasted almost two minutes.

After I settled down, they took me to another room and said, "Wait here for an hour, and we'll come and get you."

I was glad to have some time to rest after that painful and disorienting experience. When the hour was up, they came in and took me back to the same room. I got all strapped in again so they could pour cold water in my other ear. This time was worse, because I knew what was coming.

The chilled water going into my ear hurt a lot. But I remembered that when I was growing up and had to go to the doctor to get a shot or something, Mother would tell me, "If something hurts, you just sit and take it quietly." And that's what I did.

All week long, the medical people put us through the tests without telling us anything about what each test was for. I read later that the guys often asked why they were having a particular test and were either ignored or told it was too difficult to explain or that they didn't need to know why. The women didn't ask, probably because we just wanted to do our best and didn't need to know the details. I did read about some of the tests later, and found that the water-in-the-ear test was to see if the vestibular systems—the body's balance mechanism—in each of my ears worked the same. If they reacted differently, it could indicate that my vision might not remain stable as I turned my head. In other words, I might get dizzy when I turned my head quickly to look at a problem in a spacecraft.

One more day to go. Friday started with EEGs

(electroencephalograms). In those days, they didn't use little stickers to attach the wires like they do today. Each wire ended with a needle that was inserted into my skin. The nurse stuck eighteen needles in my head with wires running from them to a machine. At first, I just relaxed, and the doctor recorded my brain waves. Then he asked me to hyperventilate so he could see what that did to my brain waves. I did what he told me to do, as I had with all the tests that week. I didn't care what they told me to do, I just did it because I believed it would get me one step closer to getting into space.

Some tests that day were even stranger. In one, they stuck a large needle in the base of my thumb and then ran electricity through it. The technician said, "This is going to hurt." It did, and it made my hand jump all around. It wasn't any fun, but it told them something about how well my nerves conducted electricity and whether my muscles reacted correctly to stimulation from the nerves. They also tested the nerves in my lower arm by pressing a two-pronged electrical instrument into the inside of my forearm. I'm not sure if they even knew why they were doing all these tests. I think they were just measuring everything they could think of in case it turned out to be important.

The last test on my schedule was called a tilt-table examination. It was one of the easiest things I had done all week. At first, I just lay on my back on a bed-like platform for five minutes. Then the nurse tilted the platform so that I felt like I was almost standing straight up. A ledge under my feet kept me from sliding off the platform. She said the bed was at a 65-degree angle. She kept me that way for twenty minutes and then brought the bed down flat again, where I stayed for another five minutes. Periodically though all that time, she recorded my heart rate, blood pressure, and electrocardiogram readings. As I learned later, they used this test to see if my circulatory system was keeping my brain supplied well enough when my body changed position.

That gives you an idea of what my week of astronaut fitness tests was like. But what I just described was not the complete experience. There were too many tests to recall them all—fifty or so. The doctors took X-ray motion pictures of my heart and audio recordings of my heart sounds. They checked for tiny openings between the right and left sides of my heart by having me blow into a tube hard enough to make a two-inch column of mercury float for fifteen seconds. There were many blood tests, and sessions of psychological evaluation were sprinkled among the physical tests. The psychologist asked me many questions, sometimes repeating the same ones in different sessions. How did I feel about my parents, my friends, my church?

I barely saw Dr. Lovelace at the clinic. Several other doctors and nurses handled all the tests. Of all the doctors I met at the Lovelace Clinic, the one I felt closest to was Dr. Donald Kilgore. He became my mentor, and I stayed in touch with him until he died in 2011. He often said that the women complained less about the astronaut physical exams than the men did. He once told a reporter, "These women were extraordinary human beings. The difference between the men and women was their motivation. The women desperately wanted to go into space and they knew they had to sell themselves—they knew they had to excel to the greatest possible degree, and they did."

There were good reasons Dr. Lovelace had been chosen to oversee the astronaut physical exams. An important one was that for several years his clinic had been examining pilots of airplanes and helium balloons that could fly at extremely high altitudes. He had a good idea of the kinds of physical challenges a person would face in rare atmospheres, but envisioning a long-lasting gravity-free experience was a new consideration. That's why the tests were so extensive and unusual. After that first group was selected, and after we female pilots took the same tests, NASA developed a simpler set of examinations for later groups of astronauts. We were the guinea pigs, but it was an amazing experience.

Patience

I knew I would have to wait to find out if I passed. Twenty-five women pilots were invited to take the astronaut physicals, and only three of us had been tested so far. The remaining tests could take as much as three months, even if they could be scheduled back to back. In the meantime, I kept preparing myself as much as possible for further phases of testing. On May 17, 1961, I was able to get an orientation ride in a T-33 jet at Fort Sill.

Already aiming higher and faster!

The men astronaut candidates were all jet-rated pilots, but women weren't allowed to fly jets in those days. At least

I got to ride in the two-seater and experience jet flight in the trainer aircraft, and I also flew a simulator of the F-86 swept-wing jet fighter.

The long-awaited letter from Dr. Lovelace was dated the same day I took my first jet flight. "I am happy to say that you were one of those that were successful in passing the examination," he wrote.

Yes! I knew I could do it. I learned later that nineteen women had actually completed the tests at the Lovelace Clinic, and thirteen of us passed "with no medical reservation." That was a very good showing. Of the thirty-two men who had taken the Lovelace tests, eighteen passed. We had a higher percentage. After the men took additional physical and psychological tests, seven had been selected as America's first astronauts: the Mercury 7. Eventually, we thirteen women who passed Phase I of the testing picked up our own title: the Mercury 13.

Dr. Lovelace wrote that we would soon take part in the next phase of tests, perhaps as early as the following month. He advised us to stay in the best physical condition we could because "the forthcoming tests are going to require considerable physical stamina." That was fine with me.

Two weeks later, the twelve of us got a letter from Jerrie Cobb. She had been the first woman to pass the Lovelace tests and had since taken additional tests at the U.S. Navy's School of Aviation Medicine in Pensacola, Florida. She wrote to tell us that the rest of us were to go there next. "These tests consist of physical fitness, endurance, low-pressure chamber, acceleration, clinical examinations, airborne EEG, etc.," she wrote. This set of tests would take two weeks, and eight of us were scheduled for July 16-29, 1961. Again, she reminded us not to mention this to the press because "it could seriously jeopardize this entire research program."

It seemed strange that she reminded us to avoid publicity because a month earlier *Parade* magazine's April 30 issue had featured a story about Jan and Marion Dietrich's participation in the Lovelace tests. The article about the twins was written by Jackie Cochran, the WASP organizer who supported the women's testing. Jackie had previously warned us to keep quiet about the program. She published that article, even saying in it that "Five [women] have already passed," despite the fact that Dr. Lovelace had said everything would be kept confidential until all the female volunteers had been tested. I guess if you put money in the project, you could make or break the rules. But if they wanted me to keep quiet about the next phase of tests, I would do that.

On May 31, I sent Dr. Lovelace a letter to update him on my exercise regimen, my recent jet experience, and the fact that my flight hours were now up to 1,300. I wrote that the upcoming tests "mean quite a bit to me to help you out in your research for the program and in the future I hope our nation." I felt so fortunate and excited to be in this program and have a chance to go into space.

Wally Funk

CHAPTER 4
My Quest Continues

NOT FINISHED TESTING

A week before I was scheduled to be in Pensacola, I received a letter from Dr. Lovelace about a delay. He didn't say why, just that "It has been necessary to change the testing date to begin on Monday, September 18." Okay, that means more time to increase my endurance.

A few days later, I got a letter from Jackie Cochran, who had paid for our expenses in Albuquerque. She said that twelve women had now been invited to the next round of tests, and that she was willing to help pay the travel and meal expenses for any of us who needed financial help. She wanted to support the program even though at forty, she was too old to be tested herself. She also wrote, "There is no astronaut program for women yet. The medical checks at Albuquerque and the further tests to be made at Pensacola are purely experimental and in the nature of research." She went on to say, "But I think a properly organized astronaut program for women would be a fine thing." Of course, I thought so, too. And I was a little surprised at her saying there was no astronaut program for women yet. Everyone at the Lovelace Clinic had talked like we were being evaluated as potential astronauts. It must be some formality of language, I thought. Working for the Army at Fort Sill, I could understand technicalities like that.

In the meantime, I was already arranging for some other tests. The men's program consisted of physical fitness testing at the Lovelace Clinic (what we called Phase I), psychological and psychiatric evaluation at the Aero Medical Laboratory at Wright Field in Dayton, Ohio (Phase II), and physical stress tests at Wright Field (Phase III). Jerrie had completed the first phase in February 1960 in Albuquerque and tests similar to Phases II and III in September 1960 in Oklahoma City and May 1961 in Pensacola, respectively. It was going to be a couple of months before my Phase III tests; so Jerrie helped me schedule the psychological phase starting on August 3, 1961, at the Veterans Administration Hospital in Oklahoma City with Dr. Shurley. I was twenty-four years old now, and my flying hours were up to 4,600.

At this time, the only women I knew in the Mercury 13 were Jerrie Cobb and Gene Nora Stumbough. I had talked with Gene Nora (pronounced Jeenora) about the tests in April 1961 at a Ninety-Nines meeting in Oklahoma City and suggested she apply. I knew she had won the Top Woman Pilot award at the 1959 NIFA meet I had also done well in. And as a student at the University of Oklahoma, she was currently the school's first female flight instructor. Now I had a chance to meet another one, if only briefly. Jerrie had also helped Rhea Hurrle arrange to take the Phase II tests the same week as I would. Like Jerrie, Rhea was thirty years old. She demonstrated and delivered airplanes all over North America for the brokerage business she and her husband, Gene Allison, owned. Rhea was scheduled to do the psychological and isolation tests on Monday through Wednesday, and my tests would be Thursday through Saturday. Jerrie invited us both to stay at her home in Oklahoma City. She fixed up her spare bedroom as what she called a "space dormitory" with spaceship-printed bedspreads on the twin beds and solar system maps on the wall.

I got to Jerrie's house on Wednesday, while Rhea was still in testing. Rhea wasn't back at the house by dinnertime; so Jerrie and I went ahead and ate. We talked through part of the evening until the call finally came for Jerrie to pick Rhea up. It had been a long day for her, but neither of them would tell me anything about the tests I would be having the next three days.

Thursday and Friday were what you might expect for a psychological evaluation. The people who interviewed me wanted to know about my life, my parents, my friends, my flying, anything I loved or hated. They couldn't quite understand that I didn't have any bad thoughts in my head. I was always happy. My parents were happy. I told them about my train and erector set, and carving, and that I never had any fears. I told them about my young life and the freedom I was given. They said, "What kind of music do you like?"

Rock and roll music was popular then, but I said, "I like opera."

They said, "What's your favorite opera?"

"It's *Nabucco*," I said.

"Who wrote it?"

"Verdi."

Their mouths dropped open because I knew about operas.

All the time they were interviewing me, they were putting a thermometer in my mouth every two hours, and they would dutifully write down the results. I asked why, and they said I would find out eventually.

They gave me so many tests. On the Rorschach test, I had to describe what I saw in some ink blots. In another test, they showed me a picture and told me to make up a story about it. I had to draw a person, complete a sentence, and fill out a long form selecting my preferences about lots of things. There were tests about mathematical reasoning and understanding mechanical things. I can't remember them all. The tests tired my brain, and when I got back to Jerrie's house in the evening we would do physical exercises so I could stay in shape and unwind.

I Set a Record

At the end of the second day, they said, "Tomorrow, bring your swimsuit. We have a chamber of water that we want you to go in." The little I knew about what was coming next was what I had read in that *Life* magazine article about Jerrie's test. It was going to be interesting.

The next morning, I went to the hospital, and they told me to change into my swimsuit. They pointed to a door and told me there was a tank of water in the room it led to. They gave me two pieces of foam rubber, each about the size of a brick. I was to put one of them behind my neck and one under the small of my back, and float on the water, face up. They said, "You're going to have ear plugs to keep the water out of your ears, and the lights are going to be turned off. We want you to be very careful getting into this pool. We want you to lay there. Don't try to do anything; don't try to swim. Just lay there for as long as you can." Before I went through the door, I saw there was a clock above it. It was 8:30 in the morning. I went in, and here's this great big steel tank, about eight feet across and eight feet deep. I climbed up the steps and got in the pool.

I was going to have to stay still in the water or the foam pieces would shift out from under me. The pictures I saw in *Life* magazine of Jerrie in the tank showed that she had an inflated rubber collar around her neck and large pieces of foam rubber strapped around her hips. But I wasn't worried about these small pieces I had. I grew up swimming and soaking in the hot springs in Taos; so I was used to being in the water.

They turned the lights off, and it became absolutely dark. It was like my eyes were lined with black velvet. I couldn't see anything, and the doctors couldn't see me. It was also completely quiet in the room—not a sound. Well, that's not quite true—I could hear a tiny whisper with each breath I exhaled. I wondered if I would be able to hear my own heartbeats, but I never did. I couldn't feel any air movement. I couldn't smell anything. I spread my arms out to the sides; that seemed to make me feel most comfortable. After a couple of minutes I thought, something is wrong here. I can't feel a thing. I slapped the surface of the water, but I couldn't feel it. I patted my face with my wet hand, and I couldn't feel the water on my face. I brought my hand up and dripped water from my fingers onto my face. I couldn't feel the drops. Ah, now I realized why they had taken my temperature so often. They figured out my average body temperature and made the water and the air in that room exactly that temperature. It was humid enough that the water on my face didn't evaporate and cool my skin. I felt like I was floating in nothing. I was in space!

A microphone was hanging a couple of inches above me so they could monitor my breathing. Some people who had taken this test in the past couldn't stand the lack of physical sensations and started to hallucinate. The microphone would alert the doctors if I got into trouble and needed to get out quickly. They told me I could talk to them as much as I wanted, to share my thoughts or just have the comfort of talking to someone. I don't think I talked at all during the test. I didn't have anything to say.

I just lay there and lay there. I thought about things I had done in the past and what my future might be. I thought about being here and taking these tests, and the possibility of becoming an astronaut. I had enough money; so I wasn't worried about that. My folks had just given me a brand new car; so I thought about that. I thought about what great parents I had bringing me up. I had a horse back in Taos, and I was doing well in my flying. I was not bored lying there. I can't tell you to this day what all I thought about. I think I could turn my brain off. I just felt comfortable. My life was good, and I was relaxed. I think I dozed off a few times.

After a while, I heard a voice. One of the doctors said, "Wally, how do you feel?"

"I feel fantastic."

"Are you hungry?"

"Nope."

"Do you have to go to the bathroom?"

I said, "I already did that." My goodness, I'd been lying in a tank of warm water for several hours. What did he expect?

Then he said, "We're going to turn the lights on very slowly. Get a towel on you, and come on out. Be very careful getting over the top of the tank."

So I moved over to the place where I could reach the steps and get out of the pool. I put the towel around me and came out of the room. I turned around to look at the clock, and they had covered it up! I had no idea how long I had been in the tank. I guessed it was about four or five hours.

I went into the adjoining dressing room and put my clothes on. I came back out and sat down with the doctors. They said, "Wally, you stayed in ten hours and thirty-five minutes."

I said, "Holy cow." It didn't feel like that. It turned out that was a new record. Jerrie had stayed in nine hours and forty minutes before they told her that was long enough and she should come out. Rhea had stayed in for ten hours until they told her to stop.

I spent another half hour answering questions. Where was I, and why was I there? What did I feel while I was in the tank? Some of the questions were the same ones they had asked during the last two days. I guess they wanted to see if I had changed my mind about my parents, my school, whatever. No, I hadn't changed my mind about anything.

Jerrie, Rhea, and I had all passed a much more difficult isolation test than the male astronaut candidates had. They were just put alone in a dark, soundproof room for two or three hours. They could walk around or sit at a chair at a desk in the room. John Glenn even said later that he found some paper in the desk drawer and wrote poetry in the dark to occupy himself. Being able to do nothing but float in water that we could not feel was certainly more like being in a space capsule without normal gravity.

The Wally Funk Program

I returned to Fort Sill and stayed active the rest of August, but I was looking forward to the Phase III tests that were scheduled to start September 18. A week before I planned to leave for Pensacola, I received a telegram from Dr. Lovelace. It said,

> *REGRET TO ADVISE ARRANGEMENTS AT PENSACOLA CANCELLED PROBABLY WILL NOT BE POSSIBLE TO CARRY OUT THIS PART PF [sic] PROGRAM YOU MAY RETURN EXPENSE ADVANCE ALLOTMENT TO LOVELACE FOUNDATION C/O ME LETTER WILL ADVISE OF ADDITIONAL DEVELOPMENTS WHEN MATTER CLEARED FURTHER.*

Jerrie's assistant also sent a telegram that said,

> *MISS COBB HAS JUST INFORMED ME FROM WASHINGTON THAT SHE HAS BEEN UNABLE TO*

REVERSE DECISION POSTPONING FLORIDA TESTING AGAIN LOVELACE WILL CONTACT YOU SHORTLY BUT JERRIE WANTED YOU TO KNOW IMMEDIATELY SO YOU WOULD NOT PLAN TRIP THIS WEEKEND VERY SORRY FOR SUCH SHORT NOTICE BUT IT IS UNAVOIDABLE.

I was stunned. I was looking forward to that experience so much, and I had worked so hard to be ready for it. I didn't know the reason for the cancellation at that time, but I learned more about it later. Dr. Lovelace had been doing the women's tests without NASA's involvement. The expenses were paid by the Lovelace Foundation and Jackie Cochran and her husband, not the government. Apparently, someone had questioned whether NASA had approved the women's tests at the Naval Air Station in Pensacola and whether the costs were justified. NASA declined to authorize them, and the Navy withdrew permission to use its facilities.

I was very disappointed, no doubt about that. But I wasn't going to sit back and sulk over it. I was young and happy, and I believed I would eventually go into space. So I threw it a fish, and I went on with my life. I figured I would find an alternate path.

Nearly a year later, in July 1962, Jerrie Cobb and another Mercury 13 member challenged NASA in a Congressional hearing. The other woman, Janey Hart, was the oldest of the Mercury 13 and the wife of U.S. Senator Philip Hart of Michigan. With the help of her husband's connections, a special subcommittee of the U.S. House of Representatives' Committee on Science and Astronautics agreed to hold a public hearing to examine whether NASA had discriminated against women in the selection of Mercury astronauts. Jerrie and Janey made strong arguments, testifying about the great performance of the Mercury 13 in the Lovelace exams, Jerrie's success with the Pensacola tests, and the records she, Rhea, and I had set in the isolation tests. But NASA was a good old boy network, and they weren't going to let us in. That was the end of that.

I had no regrets. I realized I still had a lot to do and achieve. I was disappointed, but I was never bitter. I was brought up that when things don't work out, you let it pass and keep moving forward. I didn't have the Lovelace Program anymore, but I had the Wally Funk Program. I would find a way to get into space.

That fall, I relocated to California. My parents had moved to southern California by then. My father had battled tuberculosis for many years, and they were trying to find a climate that would be better for his health.

I got a job with Wright's Flying Service at the airport in Hawthorne. I had flown in and out of that airport several times, and on one visit, I asked if they needed a flight instructor. They did, and I got the job. I also flew charter flights for them and served as chief pilot of Wright's Flying Service. That meant I was in charge of logistics and personnel for the company. I had to make sure the aircraft were properly maintained and the other pilots were well trained. I was responsible for keeping up to date with state and federal regulations and making sure we were in compliance. As an instructor and charter pilot, I was flying seven or eight hours a day and loving it.

I bought myself a Stearman, a 1940s-era biplane with an open cockpit.

It had a 250-horsepower engine in it, and it was great for doing acrobatics. I learned to do all kinds of loops and rolls, and I taught some students how to do acrobatics, too. In the years since then, I have owned three other airplanes, all Cessnas—a 182, a 172, and a 150. The Stearman is still my favorite, even though I eventually had to sell it because I couldn't get anybody to work on its radial engine. Jets were becoming popular, and mechanics would rather work on a jet engine than a radial or a cylinder type of engine. Nowadays, some mechanics are happy to work on restoring antique Stearmans. Too late for me.

Me and my favorite plane, the Stearman

    Wright's Flying Service had a T-6, a single-engine plane that nobody ever flew. Made by North American Aviation, the propeller-driven T-6 had been used as a training aircraft by the American and British military. Its two seats were in separate cockpits, one behind the other. One day I decided to take it for a spin. I had to do a lot of taxiing. It was a tail dragger, which means it has two wheels near the front of the plane and a small one under the tail. On the ground, it sits with its nose higher than the tail. Other small planes have one wheel near the front and two closer to the middle; so the aircraft sits level on the ground. Once you learn a tail dragger, you pretty well know what you're doing. I took off, and it was fantastic. I went out to the beach and did loops and all kinds of maneuvers. That plane was great for doing acrobatics.

    About six months after that, a DC-3 was sitting at the Hawthorne airport. I asked for the key for it. It was a commercial airplane that could hold about twenty passengers, but I was by myself. I knew I could fly it. I went up and down the runway, just taxiing.

Finally the tower said, "When do you think you're going to take off?"

I said, "Now."

I got in position and took off. It was heavier than my little Stearman; so it took a little longer on the runway. It had more power because it had two engines, and I had to use more right rudder because the propellers both rotated in the same direction. I took off, and I was climbing up. Holy cow! I got the plane up; now I've got to get down without hurting it! I went out over the ocean again, did more maneuvers. You can't do loops in that aircraft; I just did a lot of different turns and altitude changes to get the feel of the plane.

I came back to the tower, and I said, "I want to make a couple of low passes and see how I feel with the power situation. Then I'll try to set it down, and if it's good, then I'll put the tail wheel down." The best way to do it is to have all three wheels down at the same time, but I didn't have enough experience in that heavy an airplane. I lined up with the runway and held the wings level. As I got closer, I was feeling good about being in control of the plane. I eased off on the power and touched the front wheels down. As I slowed more, the tail wheel touched down, too.

I did it. I pulled it off. I knew I could do it, but that doesn't mean I took it for granted that I would land easily. I used all my flying experience to be sure I was controlling that plane safely. The safe landing was a relief, but not a surprise.

I was young and confident, and I felt like I was capable of doing anything I wanted to do. That was my attitude about becoming an astronaut, too. The Lovelace women astronaut program was over, but that didn't stop me. I made up my mind to make my own arrangements to take as many Phase III-type tests as I could. I knew people in the military from my time at Fort Sill and my time working in Southern California. In August of 1962, I got permission to go to El Toro Marine Corps Air Station near Irvine, California, and take two tests. I was the first woman to get this permission, but it was because of my qualifications and reputation.

El Toro Testing

The first test was the Martin-Baker ejection seat test. I was wearing a flight suit, and a couple of Marines strapped me into an airplane ejection seat that was mounted on a long, almost vertical track. I pulled a support up over my helmet to keep my head held firmly against the head rest so that my head wouldn't come forward, because you could break your neck. They shot me up that pole, probably around twenty feet, and I came down with a terrible thud. I didn't realize it, but the guys knew. I would have a tremendous headache, and I could have a back compression. Well, I had never told anybody I had hurt my back skiing, trying to prepare for the Olympics. So I thought, "Uh-oh. I wonder if anything has happened here," but nothing happened. My back was fine.

I said, "Wow, you guys, I have a big, big headache."

They said, "We're going to help you get rid of that. We're going to take you to the high-altitude chamber test."

I walked into this chamber at El Toro. Two doctors came in with me. I sat at one end of the chamber by a console, and one of the doctors said, "You're supposed to punch out lights that come on and write your name and anything you want, and add some numbers on this piece of paper."

I put on an oxygen mask, and they started to reduce the pressure in the air to match what it would be at increasing altitudes. We zoomed on up there. I think it was to the equivalent of about 30,000 feet. And, boy, on 100 percent oxygen, I was feeling great. They say that breathing 100 percent oxygen is just the best way to get over a hangover or to get rid of a headache. So I was feeling great. Then came the real test.

A voice said, "Wally, take your mask off."

So I took my oxygen mask off.

"We want you to keep writing and pushing the lights."

So I was just blithely writing things down and doing my assignment, thinking I was doing a great job. Things got a little gray. I was still writing and pushing out buttons, but I didn't realize I was getting slower. Pretty soon, I heard something, but I didn't react to it.

Someone said, "Wally, put your mask on. Wally, put your mask on!"

Then a doctor came over and put it on me. Oh my, I thought. Oh my word! Color! Color was coming back. All the faces were coming back. I was amazed how my brain did not work without enough oxygen. I was back to normal.

One of the doctors said, "Do you need help getting out?"

I said, "No, I think I'm all right." I walked out and went around where they wanted to show me something.

They said, "Do you want to see a film of how you looked in there?"

I said, "Yeah!" In the film I could see myself with my mask off, writing on a clipboard. It was all scribbles, and I was writing way off the page into the air. I thought I was doing really terrific, because you feel a sense of well-being when your brain is low on oxygen. This is why a lot of airplane pilots have accidents. They have a feeling of euphoria, but because they're not getting enough oxygen to the brain to read their instrumentation correctly, they get into trouble. That high-altitude chamber test was a valuable experience for me.

Gravity at USC

The following year, I was able to arrange to take a centrifuge test at the University of Southern California. Being a civilian and being a woman, I could not have a G suit. Only men could have those things. So I called Mother up in Hemet, California, and I said, "Mom, I need your worst Merry Widow and girdle when you were a girl. Can you get those to me?"

She said, "You betcha."

So I made my own G suit out of her corset and girdle, stuffed my body in this tight little thing, and put my flight suit over it. I knew once they started to twirl me around in the centrifuge, they thought I was going to pass out within the first experience of 5 Gs. But I knew to keep the blood pushed up in my head.

A research engineer with the USC Department of Physiology strapped me in the centrifuge seat. We started the first run. I was sitting down, and it started to go round and round. Man, I was happy as a clam! I kept my head straight and steady. I had to push out some buttons, because they wanted to see how I would do. Doing acrobatics in the Stearman, I had been doing 360s (turning a full circle horizontally, almost like a centrifuge), which is about 4 Gs. I know because I had a G-meter in the cockpit. So this was no big deal to me.

We went a second run of 5 Gs. No big deal. I punched out the buttons of lights that were coming up for my assignments. We went a third run, no problem. I was feeling a little tired, but it was okay. When we did the fourth run, I don't know if the guy really hit the button and gave me a few more Gs, or if it was the same amount of Gs but my body not having a rest in between runs. I could tell I needed to keep the blood up to my brain. So I just tensed up my body and my neck, and I pushed all that blood back up in my head. Then I just kept doing my thing, and I passed with flying colors. I never told them that I had made my own G suit. It didn't come out until a *Dateline* television interview I did more than twenty years later.

I took my centrifuge test at USC in mid-March 1963. Three months later, the Soviets sent the first woman into space. Cosmonaut Valentina Tereshkova flew in orbit for three days, circling the Earth forty-eight times. It turned out to be just a publicity stunt because they didn't fly another woman into space until nineteen years later. But publicity was important during the Cold War, and we could have been first.

I knew I had what it took to be an astronaut. Sooner or later, I would get to space, with or without NASA. In the meantime, I had a life to live.

Wally Funk

Chapter 5
Adventures on Three Continents

Europe

My efforts to become an astronaut were on hold. After I had completed the activities at El Toro and USC, I ran out of other tests to try. Working at the airport in Southern California was interesting and fun, but I was looking for another adventure. I decided to travel and learn about other countries and cultures while I was young and my career was still flexible. In the spring of 1965, I told Father I wanted to get a Volkswagen camper and go see the world. My parents weren't even surprised. I was twenty-six years old and had some money saved up. Father gave me some traveler's checks, and Mother sewed a thousand-dollar bill into one of my undergarments in case of an emergency.

I quit my job at Wright's Flying Service, and I left for Europe in April 1965 along with a friend named Ann Cooper. I took my dog along, a small, black poodle I called "Little Toot." I don't know what Ann remembers from our trip—we've lost contact with each other—but these are my memories of that wonderful time.

The trip started with an airline flight from New York to Brussels, Belgium. I had a copy of the *Fodor's Guide to Europe* to help me find places to eat and stay. The only hotel in the book that I could pronounce was Le Pelican. We took a taxi from the airport and the driver said, "Where are you going?"

I said, "Is Le Pelican downtown in Brussels?"

"Yes."

"Take me there." I had no reservations; I was just traveling free. I was happy to be starting the adventure. It was so unique—all these people, and they didn't speak English. When we got to the hotel, I was so tired that I went up to my room and went to sleep. I woke up around midnight because of the time zone difference from home. I decided to take a walk; so I got dressed and went downstairs. When I went outside, I saw the storefronts all lit up. Women were sitting in windows, fanning themselves. They were half naked and were beckoning men to come in. I was in the middle of the red light district! *Oh,* I thought, *I've got to get out of here.* I went right back up to my room and packed my stuff. At eight o'clock, we left to get the camper that I had arranged to buy from a dealer in Brussels. Someone from the Volkswagen dealership had to show me how to go and get gas because the gas stations were underground.

Then I needed to go shopping. I had no utensils or anything. I parked the camper so I could figure out where to find a store. I had my dog with me, and a group of women gathered around my camper to look at her. I didn't speak French, but I found out Little Toot was a *caniche mineur*—"small poodle" in French. I said to one of the women, "Madamme, I need utensils, I need bedding. I need a pillow." I was pantomiming to try to make myself understood. "I'm from America. Where do I go to buy these?"

She said, "Ah, come." We went to the Bon Marche, which was like what Walmart is now. One of the women took care of Little Toot while I went in the store and got all the bedding, the pillow, pots and pans, glasses—everything I needed.

Using the map of Europe I had brought from America, we started our trip. On April 23, I left Brussels and drove to Amiens, France. I can remember exactly where I went and when, because every night I wrote on the "ocean" area of my map where I spent the night. I wrote to my parents often so they would know where I was and what I was doing. I also checked in with the American embassy in every country I visited.

Two days of driving later, we were at Mont-Saint-Michel. That was fabulous. I visited a medieval abbey that sat on top of a 300-foot-high granite peak just off the coast of Normandy. At high tide the place was an island, but at low tide people could walk out to it. The main street leading to the abbey was lined with tourist shops selling all sorts of souvenirs. I had to climb a series of increasingly steep stairs to reach the monastery. It was a strange combination of Romanesque and Gothic architecture. The first church was built there in the early 700s, but it had been rebuilt and added to until the 1400s. At different times, it was converted to a military fortress or a prison, but it housed a religious community again when I visited it.

For the next few weeks, we explored several European countries. I had grown up in New Mexico, which is one of the largest states in America; so I was surprised at how small and close together the European countries were. In Toledo, Spain, I had a hard time finding El Greco's house but was glad I persisted. The paintings were so much richer than the photographs I had seen. Then I crossed into Portugal, and I remember driving through the narrow streets in Lisbon. In some places, stone arches spanned the road between buildings, and my camper barely fit through them.

I loved the beach in Portugal and decided to come back there later. Coming back through Spain, I went to a bullfight in Barcelona.

In many of the countries I visited, I connected with people I knew or who were relatives of artists my parents had known in Taos. They were all very hospitable, and I sometimes stayed a few days with them, either in their house or in my camper parked at their property. That's one way I managed to take my long trip without spending much money. I called the camper my mini-mansion.

A friend helps me through a tight spot.

At the end of May, we ventured into Switzerland. I spent several days visiting some friends who lived about half an hour's drive southeast of Bern. The Hoffet family were friends of my parents, and I had gotten to know them when they visited Taos a few years before. They were great about telling me where to go and what to see in Europe. We happened to be there on Ann's birthday, and our hosts served her a magnificent, twenty-one-layer cake.

In early June, I headed back to France to fulfill a goal I'd had since I was a child. The Paris Air Show was held in mid-June that year, and I was thrilled to be there for it. The Blue Angels and Thunderbirds from the United States and teams from Italy, France, and Canada put on spectacular displays of precision flying. I loved looking at all the different types of aircraft from helicopters to jet airplanes. I talked with so many people about flying or maintaining all kinds of flying machines. It was truly a long-held dream come true.

Then we headed east and north. In Germany, on this visit

and others during my travels, I saw many contrasting sites. There were beautiful cathedrals and castles in places like Köln (Cologne) and Heidelberg. There were somber sites like the ovens in Dachau, and chilling Cold War reminders like the Berlin Wall. In one place, the wall was built right through a home. The doors and windows had been bricked in. I took a tour in East Berlin. Everything looked very bare there. It was strange to watch the changing of the guard at the war memorial with the soldiers marching in goose step.

The Scandinavian countries were next. The Tivoli Gardens in Copenhagen were great fun. In Norway, we camped on the shore of the North Sea. The Viking ships in a museum in Oslo were amazing. Then we boarded a boat for a scenic tour of the fjords and spectacular waterfalls.

Holland had the expected windmills and flowers. I found that wooden shoes weren't very comfortable, but the cheeses were delicious. Walking through the house where Anne Frank and her family hid from the Nazis for more than two years in Amsterdam made me admire her more than ever.

Driving across Belgium in late July took us to France, where we could get to England. The White Cliffs of Dover were quite a sight from the ferry crossing the English Channel. The next day, I drove to London. After seeing the usual tourist attractions in the city, I explored central and northern England and Scotland. I especially enjoyed Alconbury, England, where the Royal Air Force has a station. In Alconbury I visited a family friend who had recently flown the first F4H Phantom jet to the base, and her description of the flight was fascinating.

That fall, we went back through Germany and Austria and spent several days in Switzerland again. Then it was on to Italy in late September. I especially remember visiting Pompeii and seeing the displays of the destruction caused by the ancient volcano eruption. I hiked up the back side of Mount Vesuvius, and when I reached the top I could look down into the volcano crater and also see Naples and the bay in the distance. There were so many fabulous things to see in Pisa, Florence, Rome, the Vatican, and Tivoli. We went through Venice on our way back toward Vienna, Austria, where I had a special side trip scheduled. Ann stayed in Austria with Toot and the camper while I went off to pursue a long-held goal.

On October 24, I boarded a train headed for Russia. I wanted to go to Moscow and try to meet Valentina Tereshkova, the only woman to have gone into space at that time. This was 1965, and the space race between the Soviet Union and America was well underway. A cosmonaut and an astronaut had recently performed their countries' first spacewalks. America's Gemini astronauts were staying in orbit for a week or more. I wanted to be involved in space adventures, and meeting Valentina would be a way to share her experience in a small way.

I had my own compartment on the train, and the trip itself turned out to be interesting. At one point, the train stopped, and all the passengers were told to get off and go into the terminal. I wondered what that was all about. They took my passport away. It was a little unsettling, but I got everything back. They tried to give me shots, but I said, "No, you're not sticking me with any needles." An hour later, we were told we could get back on the train. Then uniformed officers came to my compartment and asked what I was reading. I had been told to bring only magazines that had no political content, so my *Reader's Digest* was no problem. We finally arrived in Moscow after traveling nearly a day and a half.

My third-floor hotel room was plain, which was fine because I planned to be out seeing things most of the time. I did have my own bathroom.

My next stop was the American embassy. I explained what my background was and told the embassy employee I wanted to meet Valentina. I guess I was a little naïve about how to arrange a visit with such a prominent person. They called the authorities and made the request, but the answer was *nyet*. I was disappointed, but I made up my mind I would come back to Russia someday and meet her. In the meantime, there were other wonderful things to see.

I went to the opera two nights in Moscow. The performances were fantastic, and the tickets were only eighty cents each. I saw the Kremlin and Red Square. I visited two magnificent old churches that had been taken over by the anti-religion government and converted into museums. Annunciation Cathedral, which was built in 1489, had white stone walls and nine tower domes that were covered with gold. St. Basil's Cathedral, which was built in 1560, looked like a cluster of towers. Each tower was topped with one of those domes that come to a point on top—I think they called them onion domes. And each dome was decorated in a different color and design.

I took the train back to Vienna. Just before we crossed the border from Russia to Poland, they stopped the train again and told everyone to get off. I wanted to know what was going on; so I decided to play sick and stay on the train. Men came and pulled all the shades down and said, "Just stay right there." Sure. When the guards left, I peeked underneath one of the blinds and took a picture.

They had great big forks, and they lifted each train car up and slid a narrower set of wheels underneath it and set it back down. Russia had wider tracks than the rest of Europe. I heard this was one of their ways of keeping any unauthorized train from going into their country.

After I got back to Austria, Ann and I drove into Czechoslovakia. In Prague, I visited Eva Kosloriva, the mother of one of the students I had taught to fly. When I came back to my camper, I found a crowd of people lined up waiting for their turn to see the strange dog in the vehicle. I had to wait my turn.

Satisfying my natural curiosity watching train tracks change in Russia

Who'd have thought such a small dog would draw such a big crowd?

After Czechoslovakia, we went through Hungary, where I saw many wagons on the roads but very few cars. I didn't spend much time in Yugoslavia or Bulgaria because I was looking forward to Greece.

We arrived in Thessoloniki on November 7 and didn't leave Greece until November 30. Athens was wonderful. We were there for ten days. A ceremonial guard at the entrance to the president's palace reminded me of the royal guards I had seen in London, although their hats were much smaller. I visited the Parthenon on a hill overlooking the city, and I could see the closely-spaced buildings of Athens extending into the distance.

We took a large boat to the island of Crete. I was concerned as I watched the crew wrap straps around my camper and lift it onto the boat with a large crane. I hoped they wouldn't drop it. I guess they knew what they were doing, because it went fine. Seeing the ancient ruins on Crete was so much better than seeing pictures of them in books. I saw things I didn't expect, too, like a large windmill with canvas sails. I expected that in Holland, but not on Crete. I also didn't expect to see banana trees there.

Exploring Europe in 17,000 miles.

Middle East

Turkey was the next country on our itinerary. I couldn't believe how huge the interior of the Hagia Sophia was. From Istanbul, I went to Ankara and enjoyed the Sunday outdoor market. In Nigde, a large group of friendly Turks guarded my camper while I toured an amazing underground city.

As we approached Aleppo in Syria, I could see the tops of many houses rising above the city wall. The rounded shapes reminded me of the *hornos*, or outdoor ovens, the Pueblo Indians in New Mexico used for baking bread.

Now I began to be immersed in Christian Biblical sites. Damascus, Syria, was where Paul came after a vision that changed him from a persecutor of Christians to an ardent disciple of the new church. I walked among the Cedars of Lebanon. I saw the Jordan River where Jesus was baptized. This was 1965, and the West Bank sector was controlled by Syria. That area included Jerusalem, where I visited the Church of the Holy Sepulcher. It was located where Jesus was crucified, was entombed, and rose. While I was in Jerusalem, I got my first camel ride near St. Stephen's Gate in the city wall.

I was in Bethlehem for Christmas. I went into the Church of the Nativity on Christmas Eve for a service. But it got really crowded, and I couldn't hear well. So I left and drove to a quiet place where I listened to the service on the radio. I had always listened to the Christmas service from Bethlehem back in Taos when I was growing up, but being there in person was very special.

The next day, I drove to the Dead Sea. There was a race track near the water, and I watched camel races. It was such a contrast from the holiday seasons I was used to. Back home, it would have been cold, and I probably would have been skiing.

I crossed from Syria into Jordan to see Petra. It was amazing.

Higher Faster Longer

I had to walk through a narrow passage between high rock walls for over half a mile just to get into the ancient city. The buildings were not constructed, but were carved out of the sheer, rock cliffs. The front walls of the buildings were elaborately carved. I climbed a steep trail to a monastery carved into another red stone cliff. It was a difficult climb, but well worth the effort.

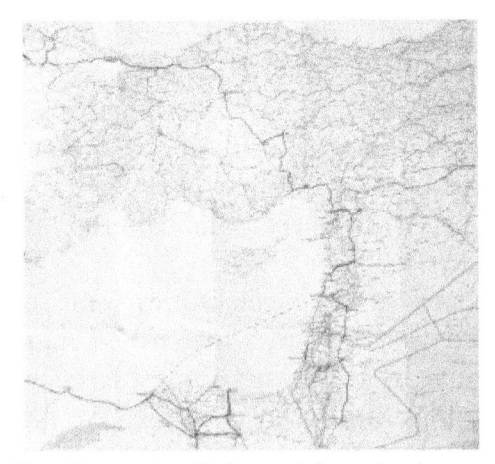

Traveling not just higher and faster, but longer and farther, too! 3,000 miles through an edge of Asia.

Africa

Our next destination was Egypt. The first night, I camped on the edge of the Mediterranean Sea at Port Said. It was beautiful.

Of course, we headed to Cairo, where I enjoyed the antiquities museum. The pyramids at Giza were next. I was amazed at how big they were and surprised that the Sphinx was smaller than I expected. I went on to see the Karnak temples at Luxor. Camels seemed to be everywhere. The Egyptians sold camel meat in the market, like we would sell beef back home. Naturally, I had to try some. It tasted a lot like beef, but it had a slightly different flavor.

I had always heard so much about the ancient ruins in Egypt, Greece, and Italy, but I was surprised by the beautiful structures in Libya. Continuing the trek across North Africa, we crossed into Tunisia. On a side trip to the island of Djerba, my little camper barely fit on the ferry. Again, locals gathered around the camper to see what it was like and were fascinated by my dog. We set up camp on the beach, and a herd of goats passed close by. Little Toot carefully ignored them.

After crossing Algeria, we entered Morocco, and I was surprised to see flamingos sitting in the tops of small trees. In Fes, I rented an airplane and flew over the area to get a bird's-eye view. The airport used red balls hanging on cables as their wind socks.

In Ouarzazate, a large celebration was underway with festively-dressed women and white-robed men dancing. The people were very friendly, and some of the women dressed me in a traditional Moroccan costume. We feasted on camel meat and couscous. We scooped the delicious food from a large common bowl with the fingers of our right hands.

Near Marrakech, I stopped to watch a farmer in a field walking behind a plow that was being pulled by a camel. Those animals had many uses. Marrakech was a tourist's dream town with beautiful pink buildings and long streets lined with orange and jacaranda trees. The bazaars were outstanding, and men put on a continuous show, performing antics such as dancing, playing music, telling fortunes, and doing acrobatics. I even watched snake charmers perform with three cobras. One man played a flute, another beat a small drum, and a third handled the snakes.

By March, we had reached Agadir, a modern Arab resort town on the Atlantic coast of Morocco. Friends of my family lived there, and it was a wonderful place to take a break from traveling. The fishermen gave us free sardines, and I remember that a smoked eel was only twenty-five cents. We stayed there for a relaxing three months.

By mid-May, the weather was changing, and I was getting restless. We drove up to Ceuta, a Spanish town just above the northern border of Morocco. From there, we caught a ferry to Gibraltar and headed back to Portugal for the second visit I had promised myself.

During the next several months, we camped in many places along the beaches of Portugal. I loved the beaches and living in the fishing villages. The men would go out in a rowboat to place a large net in the sea. They used pig skins for buoys. Then the women would go to the beach and help haul in the nets with the catch. When the fishing was done, a team of oxen would pull the boat out of the water and up on the beach.

At the end of August, 1966, we took my camper onto a freighter bound for Africa. The voyage lasted five weeks. It wasn't a fancy cruise ship, but the crewmen were considerate and gallant. It was great fun.

Part way through the voyage southward along the western side of Africa, we stopped on the coast of Angola. We were there long enough that the captain told me I could go on my first African safari. Seeing the jungle animals was fantastic, but I would see even more on later excursions. Back on board ship, we sailed around South Africa and up the eastern coast, finally landing in Mozambique.

We left the ship in Lourenco Marques, the capital of Mozambique. The city is now called Maputo. The first thing I did was sign up for a safari in Kruger National Park, just across the border in South Africa. That was fantastic. I was able to drive around the park however I wanted. I watched a baboon eat an orange. I was fascinated by the spiraled horns of a kudu buck that crossed the road in front of me. I watched graceful gazelles and sturdy wildebeest. Once, a giraffe was running beside the road, and I drove along trying to keep up with him. I saw lots of wild animals, and a huge bull elephant even snorted at me as he led his herd toward the road. I parked and went behind some bushes so I could take a picture of the herd crossing not twenty feet in front of my camper.

Continuing into South Africa, we took a tour of a gold mine in Johannesburg. I had a wonderful time going underground and seeing how the gold was mined. Wearing miners' boots and a lanterned helmet, we rode a small elevator down the 5,678-foot shaft like the old miners did. It was rather eerie, but the digging and processing were very interesting. I learned that for many years the miners had worked by candlelight, which could have caused an explosion if they had hit a pocket of methane.

From there, we drove southwest to Kimberley. Some South African friends had arranged for us to be guests of the De Beers Diamond Mines. We visited the "Big Hole," where most of the famous diamonds have been found, including the Cullinan diamond that weighed more than 3,000 carats. Again, I found the mechanical aspects of mining history fascinating. There was an old steam engine that was used to crush rock that was then run through a greased roller. The diamonds stuck to the grease, separating them from the rock.

By the time we reached Cape Town, I had traveled for twenty months, covering 45,000 miles in thirty-nine countries of Europe, the Middle East, and Africa. Cape Town was a real paradise, and it was a good place to settle for a while. The city spread among lush mountains and snow-white beaches, and there were lovely gardens and parks everywhere. The people were very kind and hospitable, and there were many opportunities in the Cape area. I gave flying lessons and flew people to outlying areas where they would go on safaris. Ann and I also did some house sitting.

With my flexible work schedule, I was able to enjoy adventures around South Africa while living in Rondebosch, a community a few miles south of Cape Town. Some friends of the Taos artists lived there, and we stayed with them. We slept in my camper, and our hosts very kindly brought meals out to us.

I loved seeing all the wild animals in their natural South African habitats, but I had a couple of special animal encounters. Once, I rode a crocodile.

Being a cowgirl comes in handy all kinds of ways!

All I had to do was come up behind it, put my hands over its eyes, and climb on. It was a pretty smooth ride. Riding an ostrich in a race was not so smooth. I was holding onto the wings so hard, they made dents in my fingers. I discovered that ostrich eggs are so tough I could stand on one without breaking it. I bought one for twenty-five cents, blew the contents out so I could save the shell, and cooked the egg. It was enough for five people's breakfasts.

Christmas in 1966 was interesting because it was the middle of summer in Cape Town. I shared a turkey dinner with friends. To avoid the heat, we dined late Christmas Eve around their lovely garden and pool.

Wally Funk

Back on the Road

The urge to see more of Africa finally led me back on the road. From Cape Town, we drove along the famous Garden Route of South Africa. The winding drive took five days through an expanse of beautiful protea flowers, forests of stink wood, and white-sand beaches at Port Elizabeth. From there, the road veered away from the coast until an hour or so before we got to Durban. I had a great time there. At the Durban Wings Club, I got to fly a Tiger Moth, a 1930s De Havilland biplane that reminded me of the Stearman I had owned in California.

Farther up the southeast Africa coast, we headed inland into Swaziland. As I got near the capital city of Mbabane, I was startled by two huge, white rhinos that were casually crossing the highway. Knowing that rhinos are nearly blind but will charge at the sound of a dropping pin, I gingerly edged up to them and took photos of them from just ten feet away. They were busy eating their morning grass and paid no attention to me.

Then we went up to Rhodesia, which is now called Zimbabwe, and stayed with other friends there. I found it one of the most peaceful and well-run countries I had visited so far. Rhodesia had declared its independence from the United Kingdom in late 1965 and was still under economic sanctions ordered by the United Nations when I was there. The sanctions only made Rhodesia stronger by forcing its people to use their own ingenuity and natural resources. I was overwhelmed by the hospitality and kindness of these people, white and native.

While we were in Rhodesia, I was interviewed on television. It was unusual for a young American woman to be on a road trip there, and they were interested in hearing about my travels.

We finally came to the Zambezi River, which defined the border between Rhodesia and Zambia. There I saw the spectacular Victoria Falls from the air and from land. The falls produced a mighty roar and a huge spray. That's why the natives called it "the smoke that thunders." The falls were surrounded by a lush jungle except for the wide Zambezi with crocodiles and hippos basking in the sun along the river banks. Islands of hyacinths floated in the river until it plunged over the falls.

I went into Zambia just long enough to visit the famous Livingstone Museum, which was about five miles from the falls. I saw recreated villages of several different tribes in the country's history. The museum also told the story of Dr. David Livingstone, the nineteenth-century Scottish explorer who had been the first white person to see Victoria Falls.

Back in Rhodesia, we went to the capital city of Salisbury, which is called Harare today. I visited some friends there. Then we went into Malawi. It took five days to drive the 482 miles through the length of Malawi. Many times I had to make my own tracks, and I didn't see lorries (trucks) for days, much less a car. There were only primitive villages of native people along the road. I had to carry food and twelve extra gallons of petrol because supplies were so far apart. For safety, I tried to find either a government rest house or Peace Corps workers along the route to spend the nights with. This was another country that had become independent recently. It was not as well organized as some other African-run countries we had visited, and its government recognized that it still needed help and guidance from England.

When we left northern Malawi, we were in Zambia near the border with Tanzania. I wanted to cross into Tanzania, but the border guard had other ideas about letting tourists in. I had been told I could obtain a visa and visitor's pass at the border, but the border official said I couldn't go in. All I could do was turn around and try to find help in Lusaka, the capital of Zambia.

The trip there was along 670 miles of terrible dirt road that lorries had used to carry oil from Dar es Salaam to the Copper Belt. Now it carried very little traffic, and I sometimes had to stop and cut bushes out of the road. That trip was no picnic, but we finally made it to Lusaka. I had to stay there two weeks to get my visa and visitor's pass. We went back to the Tunduma, Tanzania, border post, only to find that the same border official still refused us entry. This time, the "color of my skin was wrong." Other whites were being turned away as well. I was discouraged and turned back to Lusaka again, but this time I had another problem—petrol. There was no such thing as a gas pump on that desolate, primitive road, and I had used my extra gas to get to Tunduma. By begging and borrowing from store keepers and the Italian pipeline workers, I managed to get two to ten gallons of petrol at a time to get back to Lusaka. The local water was not drinkable; so we had to ration our five-gallon supply of water.

I needed to come up with a new plan. I decided to drive back through Salisbury, Rhodesia, on to the port city of Beira in Mozambique, and take a ship to Mombasa, Kenya. Before we got to Salisbury, though, two cylinders of the VW camper's engine lost power in Chinhoyi. We managed to get the vehicle to Salisbury, where we could find mechanics to work on it. It took a few days, but they were able to get the engine fixed. People took us into their homes and fed us while we were waiting for the camper to roll once again. This was very heart touching, and I will never forget the kindness of the people of Salisbury.

Eventually, we got to Beira and boarded the ship. Along the way, the ship stopped in Dar es Salaam and the nearby island of Zanzibar. The five-day voyage was relaxing, and I especially enjoyed having a hot shower with clean water, hot food, and a safe place to sleep. Traveling in East Africa had not been so easy. When we arrived in Mombasa, my dog was cleared through customs right away, but it took the camper, Ann, and me an extra day. Then my safari could begin.

Driving to Nairobi, I was startled and delighted to see graceful giraffes, ostriches, and elephants right alongside the highway. After visiting the sights of Nairobi, we headed northwest. At Lake Nakuru, I saw a thorn-tree forest and the spectacular sight of thousands of pink flamingos on the water. We crossed the equator at an elevation of 9,109 feet. The lush green scenery of tea and coffee plantations, first in Kenya and then in Uganda, as well as bamboo forests and the Mountains of the Moon in Uganda were incomparable. Beautiful flowers and vastness of greens at every turn in the road were unforgettable.

In Uganda, I visited Murchison Falls on the White Nile River. It was very different from the Victoria Falls I had seen in Rhodesia. The Murchison Falls are narrow, a little over twenty feet wide, but still had huge amounts of water cascading down. At Lake Albert and farther to the south at Queen Elizabeth Park, I saw lakes filled with pink flamingos and all the game I could imagine. There were magnificently-colored birds of every size, thousands of elephants, giraffes, hippos, zebras, kudu (antelopes), gazelles, buffaloes, and a number of lions, all roaming the open plain or bush.

We continued south into Rwanda and were interested in visiting the Congo, but I was advised against the trip as merciless killing of whites was still going on at the borders. In order to have a safe place for the night, we would camp near a white school master or a missionary. It was better to be safe than sorry.

We finally made it into Tanzania, entering from the northern border with no problems. This was where tourists on safaris and movie people entered from Nairobi; so the border was more open than the southern border had been. This is where I had my most thrilling safari of all, visiting the famous game park of Lake Manyara, which was well known for its lions resting in trees, and Ngorongoro Crater with its vast plains filled with wild, roaming game. Once, I parked under a tree and watched a lion that was sleeping above me. Another time, I watched two lionesses stalking a huge beast and having it for lunch.

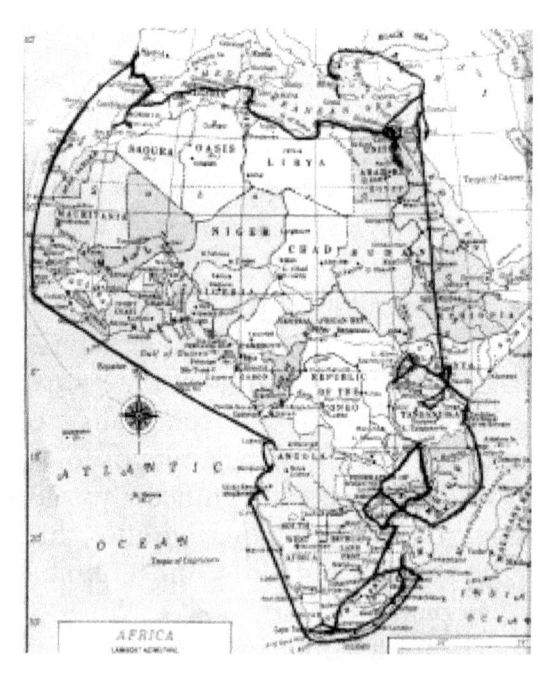

I enjoyed Africa for a year and a half, sometimes driving and sometimes sailing off the coast.

Eventually, it was time to end our African adventure. We decided to tour Israel on our way back to Europe. When we had visited Jerusalem and Bethlehem before, the West Bank territory was held by Jordan, and we had not been allowed to cross into Israel. Now, the Six Day War had just ended, and the Suez Canal was closed. So I couldn't ship the camper back to

Higher Faster Longer

Europe. I sold it, and we flew to Tel Aviv, which was a bustling, modern, skyscraper city. One of the tours I took there was a boat trip around the Sea of Galilee and Capernaum. My group was the first tourists in nineteen years to see this area overlooking Syria. It had been too dangerous between the Arab-Israeli War of 1948-49 and the Six Day War of 1967.

From Israel, we flew back to Switzerland, where I revisited my friends, the Hoffets. Poor Little Toot was getting old by now, and she died. We buried her there in Steffisburg. During July and August, we took care of the Hoffets' house while they traveled. Then some friends from California arrived, and we toured parts of Europe with them. We ended up in Brussels, where I used the money from the sale of my camper to help purchase a new, 1968 VW camper. Ann and I took it onto a Yugoslav freighter that was sailing for New York.

I felt the two and a half years I had spent in Europe, the Middle East, and Africa slipped by quickly. But I had traveled 80,000 miles in fifty-nine countries. I had collected a wealth of knowledge and experienced many kinds of places and events. I had seen the struggles of people in some other parts of the world and witnessed some well-intentioned but often misplaced American aid. During the trip, I had followed my curiosity into unfamiliar territory. I had always been self-confident, but this adventure had reinforced that. And more than ever, I was proud and grateful to be an American.

Wally Funk

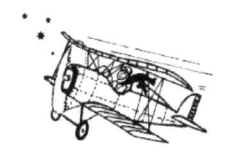

CHAPTER 6
I Look at Flight from Both Sides Now

AMAZING AMERICA

The life of a sightseeing nomad was fascinating and fun, but after two and a half years, it was time for me to settle down and build a career. I was twenty-eight when I returned to America at the end of September 1967. It was good to be back. On the way to my home in Southern California, I decided to see as much of the United States as I could. My "Mini-Mansion II" and I crisscrossed the country on a leisurely excursion.

One of the most memorable places I visited early in the American tour was Cape Kennedy in Florida. I toured NASA's launch facilities and marveled at the size of the massive Vehicle Assembly Building that was built to assemble the Apollo/Saturn vehicles. I happened to be there on January 22, 1968, and watched the launch of Apollo 5.

That unmanned flight conducted the first in-space test of the ascent and descent engines of the lunar module that would carry astronauts to the Moon's surface. Even though I was ten miles from the launch pad, I could hear the roar of the rocket engines, feel the vibrations in the ground under my feet, and watch the rocket rise and the second stage ignite. My desire to fly into space was as strong as ever.

Someday, I'm going to be on one of those.

As I traveled on, I found the sites in America very different from what I had seen in all those foreign countries, but still fascinating. Colonial Williamsburg in Virginia reflected the early days of this country. Cypress Gardens in Florida showcased our tropical landscape. The French Quarter in New Orleans and my own home town of Taos demonstrated our multicultural heritage. The Grand Canyon in Arizona was a vista like no other I had seen anywhere.

When I got back to Hawthorne, in southern California, I called on Mr. Wright. He was happy to hear from me and hired me back to my previous job as chief pilot with Wright's Flying Service. I had been able to do some flying and flight instruction during my travels, but now it was great to get back into doing those things daily. And being fully employed, I could afford to expand my flight experiences in my spare time.

I had gotten my glider license at Oklahoma State, and now I was able to enjoy that sport again. I would hitch a ride into the air by attaching my glider to an airplane with a long cable. The airplane towed me to pick up speed and lift. I would get airborne and then detach from the tow plane. Then I would soar silently and feel free, flying like a bird. It was so wonderful

I wanted to help other people enjoy it; so in 1970 I earned a commercial glider rating that enabled me to teach others how to fly a glider.

My parents were still living in southern California, and I would go to visit them in Hemet, which was a couple of hours' drive from Hawthorne. I loved hang gliding off the cliffs near Hemet and soaring out over the beautiful lake there.

First Lady Inspector at the FAA

In 1971, my spirit of adventure led me to apply for a job as a bush pilot in Alaska. I'd be flying in rough terrain where there weren't any landing strips. I would have to modify an airplane with extra-large tires, skids, skis, or pontoons to land wherever I could find a level stretch. I would meet adventurous people like hunters, missionaries, rescue workers, and people who live in isolated areas. I knew a man who worked for the FAA (Federal Aviation Administration); so I asked if he would write me a letter of recommendation. He called me and said, "Wally, why don't you come into my office on Monday?"

From the way he spoke, I knew to be dressed up when I went. On Monday, I sat down in his office, and he said, "How much do you know about the FAA?"

I said, "Well, I'm a flight instructor. I go by all the rules. I've had excellent performance, with all my students passing the first time. I've seen you guys out in the field working. I've been to your office getting my licenses. I know your guys."

He said, "How would you like to come and work for us?"

Oh my goodness, I thought, *that takes an awful lot of education. I don't know if I can do that.* Then I caught myself. *Of course, I can do that.*

"Absolutely," I said.

Later, I had an interview with several FAA people, and I

answered all their questions. Then I asked them about what they expected of me and what my future would be with the FAA. One of the interviewers, Bill Glenn, said, "I like your line of questioning. You're hired." Bill became my first boss at the FAA. And I became the first woman hired as an FAA inspector.

My job started with completing the FAA General Aviation Operations Inspector Academy course in Oklahoma City.

First woman graduate of the FAA Inspector training course

The course lasted five weeks, totaling 200 hours of instruction in pilot certification, flight testing procedures, and investigating accidents and violations.

Then I settled in at my new office in Santa Monica, California. One of my responsibilities was to handle aviation-related complaints. They ranged from reports of aircraft buzzing houses to inquiries from homeward-bound commuters about helicopters they saw from the freeway. One driver actually thought the helicopters were following him every day until I explained that his freeway hours coincided with the radio and television traffic reporting.

Another thing I did was supervising private pilot written

exams. I'd get the clock out and say, "Start, and don't stop until you're finished. Then give me your paper." That wasn't the most exciting part of the job, for sure, but it was important.

Inspecting flight schools was more interesting. I had to check their instructors and chief pilots to make sure they were doing everything correctly. I inspected their airplanes to make sure they were in perfect shape and that all the paperwork was in order.

I enjoyed giving check rides even more because it got me into the air. When someone wanted to qualify for their private or commercial pilot license or a particular rating like instrument or multi-engine, I would ride with them. I would sit in the right seat and watch them perform all of the maneuvers that were required for that license or rating.

Another responsibility was investigating aviation accidents that involved any part of an airplane not being flyable or not being safe to fly. The FAA generally investigated nonfatal accidents, but I could also go and watch National Transportation Safety Board (NTSB) investigators work at sites of fatal or high-profile accidents.

The work program of an inspector was normally an 8:00 A.M. to 4:30 P.M. job, but sometimes I was out in the field or on an accident inspection for days at a time. It was exciting to drive to work every day because no two days were alike. Job training was taking place all the time. About once each year, I was sent back to Oklahoma City for refresher courses on subjects like hazardous materials or accident prevention. Sometimes we would also have courses in our own Western Region, which made it convenient. Like the old saying goes, "When you think you know everything there is to know about flying, you had better hang up your hat, because a lack of knowledge will bite you."

In 1973 I was promoted to the position of specialist with

the FAA's Systems Worthiness Analysis Program (SWAP). In that position, I conducted inspections of air taxi services, airplane charter services, and airplane rental operations. I had to determine that their aircraft were properly maintained and their office operations were done correctly. My area included Arizona and Nevada as well as California.

This deep involvement with all aspects of airplane operations seemed to feed my enthusiasm for all kinds of aviation activities. In 1972, I made my first parachute jump. It was in the desert in Southern California. When I told my secretary at the FAA what I was going to do that weekend, she said, "Don't you go hurt yourself."

"I won't," I said. I was confident because I knew how to pay attention to instructions. Before I jumped, I would know exactly what to do. I guess you could say I'm a responsible person, but a risk taker—up to a point.

I love being up in the air, even if I'm falling through it!

I was with a group of other first-time jumpers. We practiced getting in and out of our harnesses, how to climb out of the airplane, and how to arch our backs and spread our arms and legs after leaving the plane. Finally, after all the practicing, we got in the aircraft and took off.

I took my first parachute jump, and I loved it!

I went right back up and took another one. I was using a big, round canopy with alternating red and white sections. Today, they use much smaller parachutes in different shapes. I would love to try that. Twenty years later, I went skydiving a couple of times. I did some hot-air ballooning, too. If it was up in the air, I loved it.

In 1974, I tried a different kind of flying. One of the Goodyear Blimps was based between Hawthorne and Long Beach. I knew the pilot; so I went down to see it. I got in the cockpit with him, and we took off.

Straight up and down like a helicopter, but at a more leisurely pace

I got to fly it, probably twenty or thirty minutes. I remember it was very loud, because the engines were so close. We went straight up, which an airplane doesn't do, and then we started going forward. It didn't go very fast, maybe five to ten miles an hour. It was a lot like flying an airplane, except for taking off and landing vertically. It was fun.

It was about this time that my father died at the age of seventy-seven. He was a good father to me, and I knew I would miss him. But I also knew he was now in a better place. I had always been closer to my mother, and knowing my relationship with her would continue was comforting.

First Lady Investigator at the NTSB

But back to the FAA. I never set my sights on applying for a job for the purpose of breaking some barrier or glass ceiling. I just wanted to move into the next phase of my career. I was glad to be the first female FAA inspector, though, because that opened the door for other women. By the end of the 1970s, there were at least five other women FAA inspectors working in Alaska, Hawaii, California, Texas, and Florida.

I wasn't expecting it, but in December 1974 I was asked to make another "first woman" move. As an FAA inspector, I worked closely with the Los Angeles National Transportation Safety Board team. I was responsible for investigating nonfatal general aviation accidents. I would write up reports and send them to the NTSB. They would review my report and make a determination of the probable cause of the crash. Sometimes I observed and helped the NTSB team with their investigations of fatal crashes, too.

Apparently, the NTSB guys liked the way I worked, because one of them called me and said, "How would you like to come to work for the NTSB?"

"Are you kidding?" I said. "I don't have the knowledge you guys want."

"We'll train you," he said.

"Okay," I said. It was that simple. I was extremely lucky. I would be the first female among the nation's sixty-eight male NTSB Air Safety Investigators. That's probably what got me a special invitation a few months later. I opened my mail one day and found a formal-looking card with embossed script that said, "Mrs. Ford requests the pleasure of your company at a brunch to be held at the White House on Monday, June 23, 1975 at 12 o'clock." It was very nice, but I had no idea why I was invited. I took it to my boss, Al Crawford, and I said, "What do you reckon this is?"

Al said, "That is an invitation to the White House. You're going to go to D.C., and you're going to go to the brunch."

The brunch turned out to be a "Women's Federal Forum." It was a lovely event held in the State Dining Room. I never expected to have a meal in the White House.

I had been in Washington, D.C., five months before that for my first NTSB assignment. I attended a five-week introductory investigations course. I began learning the mechanics of dismounting moveable parts and studying the relationship of one part to another to figure out just what caused each crash. The point of investigating every air fatality was not to assign blame, but to identify the cause and educate other pilots so they could prevent it from happening to them.

The training never ended. I went to five schools a year. I went to every engine school, propeller school, every maker of major parts like engines, starters, and alternators. There was a lot to learn, and it was challenging. For example, just between January and April 1976, I attended a training school for Lycoming engines, a training school for the Cessna 400 Series, and a legal and engine accessories course. The following year, I learned about Allison engines and attended the Bell JetRanger Helicopter School. Learning to fly a helicopter was another type of piloting I really enjoyed experiencing.

This little helicopter I flew at Fort Sill in 1960 was pretty basic compared to the newer JetRanger.

The next year, it was the Cessna Citation Jet School, the Piper Aircraft School, the Lear Jet School, and the GE engines factory. In 1980, one school I attended was for the Mitsubishi MU-2 turboprop aircraft. Those schools were important for learning about the equipment and also for getting to know people whom I could call during an accident investigation and ask for their help with evaluating a damaged part. There were always new and refresher courses for how to do investigations, too.

In January 1975, I had just gotten back to my new office next to Los Angeles International Airport after completing my introductory investigation course in Washington when I got my first field assignment. I assisted the investigator in charge, Guy Moshier, with a midair collision that killed twelve people in a De Havilland plane and an instructor and student in a Cessna 150. The Cessna had smashed headlong into the left side of the commuter transport's cabin. The smaller plane tore off the De Havilland's left wing and disintegrated on impact. The larger plane's right wing then collapsed under stress, and the cabin plunged to the ground.

I loved flying, and seeing the tragedy of people dying in

airplane crashes was sad. Especially because, as I would come to find out, so many of the accidents and deaths could have been avoided by pilots simply being more careful and more observant.

During my first two years with NTSB, there were three midair collisions in the Los Angeles area. It was a fairly congested airspace, with several busy general aviation airports. The interesting thing about all three of those crashes was that they all occurred during "severe clear." I mean, the weather was beautiful and completely clear. The pilots were flying VFR (visual flight rules), which meant they weren't being supervised by air traffic controllers. It was up to them to watch for other aircraft near them. In all three cases, there was no reason for the occupants of either plane not to see the other, although in one case the sun was setting and might have blinded both pilots.

After one midair accident, a surviving pilot told me he was flying and saw something white flash by and felt a thump. A Cessna 210 flying in the opposite direction had clipped the engine mounted below the right wing of his Beechcraft 200. That engine began leaking fuel and trailing smoke. He shut it off and managed to land safely at John Wayne Airport in Orange County. The right wing of the Cessna was badly damaged, and the aircraft plunged to the ground, killing both occupants.

After another midair accident, the surviving pilot said his Cessna 152 was climbing when suddenly he felt a flash and a bump and his door flew open. His airplane was hard to control, but he was able to guide it to a landing at Van Nuys Airport. A Piper Cherokee had hit his left wing and landing gear from behind. The Piper lost a wing and crashed into the roof of a department store, killing all three people aboard. Again, the people in the two aircraft simply didn't see each other.

In May 1975, I got my first assignment as investigator in charge of a fatal accident. A Lockheed Super Constellation had crashed in Mesa, Arizona, killing all six people aboard. I knew I was a rookie; so I worked extra carefully. The airplane was about twenty years old and had just been converted for use as a crop duster. The fatal flight was supposed to deliver the plane to new owners in Canada after a stopover in Kansas City. Just after taking off from Falcon Field in Mesa, three of the four engines lost power. The Constellation skimmed just over the rooftops of a residential facility for children who had been separated from their families. Then it smashed through a tree, took the roof off a small building, and hit the ground. It skidded to within fifty yards of a house where a family was having a Mother's Day barbeque. The fully-fueled plane immediately burst into flames. The fire was so intense that much of the aircraft melted.

The debris was scattered over a 300-yard path. My team and I spent a couple of days searching for any pieces that could provide a clue to how the crash happened. It was an awful scene, but I was glad that no one on the ground was injured.

As the airplane had taken off, smoke had trailed from the number two and three engines. The co-pilot and the flight engineer were inexperienced with that type of aircraft. They made the mistake of feathering the plane's number one engine, which was operating correctly. Feathering the engine meant that they rotated the propeller blades to be parallel to the air flow. On an engine that was not operating, that would decrease drag and help the airplane maintain speed and altitude. But feathering an operating engine left it powerless to propel the plane. That left the Constellation with only the number four engine working, and the aircraft fell to the ground. A simple preflight task like refueling the fire retardants for the engines, which hadn't been done, might have saved that plane.

Unpredictable

My NTSB job was anything but predictable. Accidents didn't happen on a regular basis. I might go a month without having an accident to investigate, and the next month I might have two. There was one particularly grueling, five-week period in 1980 when we had to deal with a dozen crashes with a total of twenty-eight fatalities. I was getting tired of going out and seeing people thrown against the rocks because some pilot had I've-got-to-go-itis. It was sad and frustrating to see pilots' egos taking peoples' lives.

The other investigators in the LA office and I rotated on-call duties and carried electronic beepers for quick notification when an accident happened. One of us always had to be ready. It was important for an investigator to get to the scene as quickly as possible while the evidence was still fresh and undisturbed. We were assigned to cover California, Arizona, Nevada, and Hawaii. I was on twenty-four-hour call fourteen days a month. I had the weekend duty as either primary or secondary. If the primary went out, then the person in the number two spot went to number one. I was on the road about every third or fourth day.

I always had three gear bags in my car, ready to go: one with shorts and a T-shirt for going to places where it was warm, one for sites where the temperature was moderate, and one with heavy clothing for cold weather. One crash I investigated at Tioga Peak in the Sierra Nevada Mountains of Central California was at an elevation of 11,000 feet, and the temperature was eleven degrees below zero. I bundled up for that one.

I would get out to a crash site the best way I could. In the earlier days, we were able to fly our own airplanes out. But when President Jimmy Carter was in office, he made us go by airline, or we had to drive. This was a cost-saving measure because the economy was bad, with high inflation and slow economic growth. It had been a lot easier and faster when we could fly ourselves, but you do what you have to do.

Regardless of how I got to the general area of a crash, getting to the actual site was sometimes a real challenge. I had to try everything including hiking, riding a horse, riding a mule, being dropped in by helicopter, rappelling down a cliff, and going in by boat.

When I got to the site, I had to make sure the local law enforcement officers had secured the scene. I needed to see and record where every bit of debris was and where there were marks of contact with other objects, including buildings, posts, trees, vegetation, and the ground itself.

You need curiosity, patience, and a deep knowledge of aircraft to sort this kind of debris.

I learned to take photographs from overhead if possible and photograph every piece from ground level. I would survey the scatter of the wreckage and make sketches of where all the parts were. If there were any witnesses, I would interview them.

If there had been a midair collision, things got more complicated. I would have to find all the pieces of wreckage and then identify which airplane each piece came from. Examining the scatter would also add important information about the path of each aircraft at the time of collision.

One case comes to mind that shows just how hard it is to find all the debris at a remote crash site. A plane carrying an illegal drug shipment went down in southern Arizona, and the aircraft virtually disintegrated. There were only a few large pieces left. I had to go back to the crash site by helicopter five times before I finally found the million dollars in cash and the bags of cocaine that had been stashed aboard. The DEA folks were happy when I found those.

After a crash scene had been thoroughly examined and documented, I would arrange to bring all the aircraft parts back to our warehouse for examination. I might also check weather charts for the time of the accident and talk to radar controllers in the area. I would get the history of the aircraft—things like how it had been maintained, how often it flew, whether it was stored outside or in a hangar. If the accident had been a midair collision, we might use similar aircraft over the same area at the same time of day under similar weather conditions to recreate the circumstances just before the collision occurred. Finally, when I was confident I had thoroughly analyzed all the information, I would type up a report on a Selectric typewriter. The report would describe how I came to my conclusion about how the crash happened and include any suggestions I had for preventing a similar event in the future.

I had to be very thorough with the field examination. It was important not to miss anything that might be relevant. It would take extra time and money to have to return for another look. Sometimes, I had to dig for parts because they would be buried by the impact. I remember one case in Gypsum Canyon in Orange County where a light plane hit the ground under full power. The engine bored four feet into the ground.

I even took Mother on a few field investigations, and she

would search and help dig things out of the ground. She loved what I was doing in aviation and was more than happy to share it with me when she could. I didn't take her to the really bad ones, though.

I saw some pretty gruesome things. Sometimes the coroner wouldn't get all the remains of those killed in the crash, and I would have to pick them up. The other NTSB investigators I worked with had all been investigators in the military; so they had seen tragic scenes before. I quickly learned that I couldn't let emotion get in the way if I was going to do the job right. The NTSB didn't hire another female investigator for five years after I was hired. I joke that it was because they kept waiting for me to throw up at an accident. I never did.

There were some crashes where parts of the aircraft had already been stolen, even though officials were on the scene almost immediately. All the copper wiring was stripped from one plane, and another time I saw parts of a downed craft already being used as toys by children in a nearby yard. Even charred bodies were sometimes disturbed by people ghoulish enough to hunt for whatever they could find.

Besides investigating fatal aviation accidents, NTSB also investigates high-profile incidents such as those involving commercial airlines, even if they are relatively minor. I once investigated a case where a swizzle stick struck a stewardess in the eye during a flight.

Most of the accidents I worked on were fatalities, though. Just like people, each one was different. They were all tragic, and many were downright senseless. Like the one that started with two men in a bar, daring each other to perform an aerobatic feat. They got in a plane to carry out the dares, only to crash and die on impact. What a waste.

Another time, a pilot flew a plane that was overloaded by 365 pounds into bad weather, and he became completely disoriented. He crashed into the ground less than a mile from the airport.

A helicopter pilot with the Border Patrol took off chasing goats to break the boredom and crashed into a tree.

Another man had just been fired from his job. He got drunk, stole an airplane, and flew a few feet above his former employer's property, yelling angrily out the window before he crashed. We found out later that he didn't know how to fly, but had only read about it a little. He walked away from the crash, but he had some consequences to face.

In another case, a couple of contractors were returning to a construction site in the middle of a large Indian reservation in eastern Arizona. The pilot thought it would be fun to buzz the site, as he often enjoyed doing. A witness told me the small plane flew above the space between two camper trailers about twenty or twenty-five feet above the ground with the engines sounding like they were at full throttle. Apparently, the pilot then banked the plane but misjudged his altitude. The left wing touched the ground, and the aircraft flipped sideways. Both men in the airplane died.

I remember going to the scene of the crash of a twin-engine Beechcraft Duke that was being used as an air taxi. It was flying from San Diego to Palm Springs, but it crashed roughly twenty miles before its destination, south of Palm Desert. The airplane was only a year old, and it had been properly maintained and inspected. I found a wing of the plane and the tail assembly in different places away from the main wreckage. It looked like the aircraft had broken up in the air. That wasn't too surprising, because at the time of the accident, the wind was blowing at 55 miles an hour with gusts up to 75 miles an hour. Airplanes are only designed to withstand so much stress, and they can come apart in the air when they are exposed to too much pressure. All six people aboard died in that one.

Wally Funk

One accident was impossible to investigate thoroughly. The pilot and his nineteen-year-old son were flying a Cessna 150 just off the coast of Southern California. Witnesses on land and a nearby fishing boat reported seeing the red-and-white plane crash into the water. When I got to the site, all I could find were the flight log and the aircraft maintenance record book, which had floated out of the aircraft after it hit the water. The wreckage was submerged at a depth of about 240 feet, a mile offshore. Divers couldn't get to it. A car that probably belonged to the pilot was left in the parking lot of the airport where they had departed, and the car owner and his son had not returned home. But without a positive ID, I couldn't officially say who was aboard the airplane that crashed. We would never have a definite answer unless something washed ashore that clearly identified one of them. It was one of the few cases I had where we were unable to find a probable cause.

Another time, I was investigating an accident that six people died in on Santa Catalina Island. A Lear jet overran the end of the runway, skidded on the ground, slid over a 200-foot embankment, landed in thick brush, and caught on fire. The following morning, while we were studying the crash site, a Cessna 177 crashed on the same runway when the pilot forgot to put the landing gear down. No one was hurt in that one.

A very strange thing happened with one of the accidents I investigated. A Piper Cherokee that was leaving the Lake Mead area went down. We searched the area for six weeks without finding the wreckage. The father of one of the victims took some of his son's personal items to a psychic. The psychic said that the plane had landed at an airport not far from Lake Mead, took off in a certain direction, and crashed into an odd-shaped tree. We checked with area airports and found one where someone identified photos of all three of the victims. He told us which way they had flown off. We followed that path and found the wreckage in a box canyon, next to an odd-shaped rock. The rock was the only thing the psychic got wrong.

PATTERNS

During my time at NTSB, I saw more than a few box-canyon accidents, where pilots fly blind into a three-sided canyon and crash into the far wall without being able to get enough lift to make it over the top.

More often than not, pilots who survived a crash claimed that the engine quit. I would take the engine to the NTSB testing facility in Burbank and see if it worked. One pilot claimed his engine quit before his plane scraped a parked pickup truck, crashed through the plate glass window of a business, and came out the other side of the building upside down. But my investigation proved he wasn't telling the truth. I found paint scrapings and plastic particles from the pickup deep inside one of his plane's engines. It had to have been running at the time of that collision.

The most famous crash I was in charge of investigating was in San Diego in September 1978. I got the call from the FAA duty officer. There had been a midair collision between a little Cessna 172 and a Pacific Southwest Airlines (PSA) Boeing 727. The larger aircraft had plowed into a neighborhood three miles from Lindbergh Field, where it was supposed to land. Both occupants of the Cessna, all 135 people aboard the 727, and seven people on the ground were killed.

I got to the site two hours after the crash. The police department escorted me in and introduced me to the fire marshal, because they had control of the entire wreckage. I asked if any survivors had been found yet. No. The accident scene was horrendous. I could barely breathe through the odor of burning jet fuel, flesh, and wood. There were so many bits and parts and pieces around, not only the aircraft and partial human remains, but twenty-two homes the 727 had smashed into. I just started by photographing and writing notes. I was really concerned about how I was going to put this puzzle together.

My team and I started interviewing witnesses as quickly as we could, while their memories were still fresh. I find that children up to seventeen or eighteen years old are the best witnesses, because they will give me a really good description of what they saw, without including interpretations they may have formed. Eventually, we interviewed 220 people, but none of them saw the whole thing happen.

The 727 debris was clustered around the intersection of Dwight and Nile Streets. We found the airliner's cockpit voice recorder and the instrument recorder and sent them to NTSB headquarters in Washington, DC, for analysis. Two clusters of Cessna wreckage, a couple of blocks apart, were each about six blocks away from the 727 debris. I spent weeks taking pieces out of trees and cars and rooftops, documenting what I found and where I found it. It was important to find as much as possible so we could examine wires, hydraulic tubing, fuel lines, everything.

After I had filmed, photographed, and sketched the wreckage, I had it all transported to a large hangar in San Diego. We had to try and arrange the pieces of both aircraft together to figure out exactly how they had collided. There were paint transfers on some pieces that helped with that. Trying to fit the mangled pieces together was worse than any jigsaw puzzle you could imagine. We found pieces of the Cessna's propeller embedded in the 727's right wing. The impact had ruptured fuel and hydraulic lines and set the wing on fire.

The technical support I had was wonderful. This was such a major accident that NTSB sent some staff from headquarters in Washington to help. Philip Hogue, a senior investigator, was one of them. He offered to concentrate on investigating the Cessna while I focused on information about the 727. He found out that two licensed pilots had been aboard. One was a flight instructor, and the other was a less experienced pilot who was working on getting his instrument rating. He had been practicing instrument landing approaches at Lindbergh Field.

The 727 had flown from Sacramento to Los Angeles early that morning before taking off again for San Diego. The weather was warm and clear, with visibility of ten miles as the aircraft neared the airport at about nine o'clock that Monday morning. One of the questions we had to answer was why the pilots of the two aircraft didn't see each other in time to avoid the collision.

The investigation took months to complete. I listened to the recording from the PSA cockpit up to the time of the collision. I listened to the tapes of the air traffic controllers. I saw the tapes of the radar tracking of the planes. We were lucky to have some visual evidence, too. A photographer covering a press conference a few blocks away heard the collision, looked up, and snapped a picture of the 727. Flames were streaming from the gap where a large chunk was missing from the front of its right wing. His second photo showed the aircraft about to pass behind the roof of a building in a nosedive, its body rotated so the burning right wing pointed almost toward the ground. A television cameraman who was filming the same press conference also heard the collision, turned his camera upward, and filmed the remnants of the Cessna as they fell straight down.

We found that the crew was preparing the 727 for landing when the controllers in the tower told them there was a Cessna 172 at their twelve o'clock (straight ahead of them) three miles out. The crew responded that they saw the Cessna. The tower controllers also alerted the Cessna crew about the approaching

727, but they were talking to the two aircraft on different frequencies. Because of that, the two planes' pilots could not hear each other. A collision alert system alarm sounded in the tower, but the controllers ignored it. The system had been malfunctioning, and they had gotten used to having a dozen false alarms a day.

The tower's next message to the PSA crew came about thirty seconds after the previous one. The Cessna was now slightly below and in front of the 727, one mile away. The PSA crew had lost sight of the Cessna at that point, but they didn't tell the tower. Another thirty seconds later, the tower cleared the 727 to land. Forty seconds after that, the nose wheel of the descending PSA plane hit the right wing of the ascending Cessna at an altitude of 2,600 feet. The smaller plane impacted the jetliner's wing, damaging its hydraulic and electronics systems, and broke up. The larger plane veered downward, out of control, hitting the ground seventeen seconds later.

No mechanical or weather factors contributed to the collision. Multiple human errors did. The PSA crew should have kept the Cessna in sight or told the tower when they lost sight of it. Banter in the PSA cockpit just before they were alerted to the presence of the Cessna indicated that at least some of the crew might not have been concentrating on their duties. Other PSA pilots we interviewed said they adjusted their seats for their comfort or ease of seeing the instruments instead of using the recommended reference points. If the pilot of the 727 had his seat adjusted too low, he would not have been able to see the Cessna, which was flying below him before impact. The Cessna pilot should not have changed course without communicating with the tower. The tower controllers should not have ignored the contact alert alarm, even though there had been several false alarms recently.

Besides the tower controllers, both pilots had contributed

to the tragedy. This fit a pattern I noticed throughout my career with NTSB. After investigating about 450 accidents, I put together a list of accident causes in order of their prevalence. Number one was the person operating the aircraft. I won't say "pilot," because sometimes the person controlling the airplane wasn't a licensed pilot.

One of the big mistakes pilots made in other crashes I investigated was "I've-gotta-go-itis." They were in a hurry; so they didn't take time for a proper preflight inspection. Or they thought they could beat bad weather, or they thought they were sober or rested enough. Physicians and lawyers seemed particularly prone to this kind of mistake.

The other causes, in decreasing order based on my experience, were weather, mechanical problems, midair collisions, inadequate fuel management, spatial disorientation (especially at night), alcohol or drug use, misjudgment, spins, getting into a box canyon and not having enough lift to get over the top, overshooting the landing strip, heart attacks, inflight fires, inflight breakup of the aircraft, and overloading the aircraft.

After ten and a half years with NTSB, the 450 accidents I had investigated seemed to be different in their specific details, but unnervingly similar. I felt I had seen enough tragic deaths, most of which were senseless. Using the knowledge and insight I had gained, I decided I could travel around the country and abroad and deliver the safety slide presentation I had developed. I wanted to educate as many people as I could about why aviation accidents happen and how to avoid them. I figured I could serve my aviation community best by lecturing, safety counseling, airport advising, and pilot training.

I retired from NTSB in May of 1985. During my time there, I had received an Award for Special Achievement in recognition of "sustained superior performance." I think the work I did was valuable and satisfying. Now I was ready to work for improved aviation safety in other ways.

Chapter 7
Freedom and Independence

At Home in Taos

My work with NTSB had been interesting and important, but it had also been intense, with traveling frequently and observing the fatal results of so many repetitions of irresponsible behavior by pilots or wanna-be pilots. After ten years, I was ready for a freer schedule and more time for teaching students how to fly.

The first thing I did after leaving NTSB was take time off to indulge my free spirit by visiting places I had longed to see, just as a tourist. I enjoyed the sights and rides at Disneyland and Knotts Berry Farm. I went to golf tournaments. I went biking on the Strand, a twenty-two mile trail along the beaches of Southern California. I went to Lake Tahoe and explored their ski areas. I saw the sights in San Francisco.

Then I took off on a sixteen-state camping tour, visiting airports, airplane manufacturers, and other points of interest across the country. I planned the trip to arrive in Oshkosh, Wisconsin, in late July for the beginning of the 1985 Experimental Aircraft Aviation Airshow and Convention. Attending the Oshkosh Air Show had been my dream for twenty years. I stayed for the entire eight-day event and loved every minute. The flying exhibitions were absolutely spectacular, and I learned a tremendous amount from the lectures and displays. I watched the Concorde supersonic airliner make touch-and-go landings and grand fly-bys. As an aerobatic pilot myself, I enjoyed seeing the magnificent aerobatic flying demonstrations. A spectacular tribute to Vietnam War veterans included maneuvers by a dozen P-51 Mustangs, a B-52 bomber, several F-4 Phantom fighters, and Huey helicopters. Seeing many kinds of World War II airplanes was also thrilling.

It was such a wonderful experience that I just had to share it with Mother. She flew in to join me, and we celebrated her eighty-third birthday. It was especially fun to share aviation events with her because her youthful yearning to become a pilot had not been fulfilled.

After my relaxing and invigorating travels, I returned to my home town of Taos, New Mexico, to return to the career of flight instructor. I had been teaching people to fly for twenty-five years by then.

My plan was to open a flight school that specialized in teaching mountain flying. From my years of working for NTSB, I knew many pilots were not prepared for the special problems of flying in mountainous terrain, where the weather can change quickly and the terrain affects air currents. Pilots who didn't live near mountains—people known as "flatlanders"—often didn't get above 3,000 feet altitude when they flew. If they came to a mountain area on vacation, they didn't understand how to fly in the lower density air. Taos was a perfect place to teach them. The airport was at 7,100 feet, and nearby mountains rose to over 13,000 feet. I offered a weeklong, residential training program. Working with students preparing for their private or commercial license or their instrument rating kept me busy.

I had been active in the Civil Air Patrol in California, and I immediately joined the Taos squadron. By the end of 1985, I achieved the CAP rank of captain and was qualified as a mission pilot, instructor pilot, and flight release officer. I've always enjoyed being involved with the Civil Air Patrol because it is one of the ways I can mentor young people.

Besides my aviation work, I had another reason to move back to Taos. For more than five years, I had been working on building my dream house on the mesa west of town. It was just about finished when I retired from NTSB. Now I could enjoy living in it full time.

I had started by building what I called the "little house." It had a bedroom, a sitting room, a bathroom, and a kitchen. I did as much of the construction work as possible myself. Once it was finished in 1983, I could stay in it while building the rest of the house. This house would reconnect me with my roots, because it was situated on level terrain with a beautiful view so I could relate to the spirit of Taos Mountain every day. I decided to build the house with adobe bricks, which have been used in that part of the country for many centuries. It provides very effective insulation. The bricks are made of local clay, water, and straw. The mixture is poured into wooden frames and left out to bake in the sun.

Building my dream home, brick by brick

I started an addition that I called the "big house" in 1984 and finished it a year later. I wanted it to be very energy efficient; so I made the walls double thick by placing two adobe bricks side by side.

I was told that produced an R-value of 52. New Mexico's Energy Conservation Code specifies a minimum R-value of 13 for Taos; so I could expect very low heating and cooling bills. The big house was two stories tall, with a bedroom and bath on the bottom floor. The top floor was a large room where I did a lot of entertaining. The big house was attached to one side of the little house, and I built a large unattached garage behind the big house. All together, it was 5,000 square feet.

My complete dream home, with its view of my beloved Taos Mountain.

I designed the house with my favorite architectural elements. Exposed ceiling beams, called *vigas*, protruded through the walls near the roof. I embedded decorative tiles in various places when we put a finish coat over the exterior adobe walls. A British artist I knew designed an octagonal, stained glass window that I set in the first-floor wall of the big house. I like to sign my name with a heart, and in the center of the window was a bright red heart with white wings coming out of the sides. When I eventually sold the house, I took the window with me.

When I was starting work on the big house, I had someone digging with a backhoe for the foundation and utilities trenches.

They unearthed a skeleton. The police came and removed the bones, which they later determined had been buried in 1862. Another time, I dug up some very old pottery shards. I was told they dated back to the 1600s. It was a special find for me, and I arranged the shards in a three-dimensional display frame. I've always kept that, too.

    I lived in my Taos home for two years while running my flying school. I always stressed safety to my students, especially after investigating all those crashes for NTSB. One day a woman from Texas was flying to Taos to go fishing, and I watched as she crashed while trying to land at the Taos airport. It was breezy that afternoon, with wind speeds up to fifteen miles an hour. I could tell she was going to be in trouble, because she was landing crosswind. When the wind caught her single-engine Bellanca, she veered to the right and bounced up about ten feet. Then she hit the tail of a parked Cessna 320, flipped, landed in the dirt beside the runway, and skidded about fifty feet before coming to a stop on the right side of her plane. She spent some time in the hospital, but she survived. The owner of the twin-engine Cessna was lucky, too. He and his dog had been relaxing in the shade under the front of his plane just before the impact, but they weren't injured.

Captain Wally!

In early 1987, I got my captain's bars when I signed on to fly a twin-engine passenger airplane for Sierra Pacific Airlines, which was based in Tucson, Arizona.

I've always wanted to do everything there was to do in aviation, and being an airline pilot was one of those things. I flew passengers and cargo back and forth from Albuquerque to Taos for the ski season. By the end of ski season, Sierra Pacific had been sold, and I was back to teaching private flying lessons in Taos.

Chief Pilot Again

After instructing five student pilots during the spring and summer, I took off for a camping trip through Colorado and Wyoming to enjoy the colorful show of autumn leaves on the trees. I stopped in Greeley, Colorado, and decided to visit the Emery Flight School. My flight school in Taos had enjoyed initial success, but continuing interest wasn't as great as I had hoped. So I introduced myself to the owner, Buck Bleakley, and asked if the school needed a pilot.

"We need a chief pilot," Buck said.

"I'm that, too," I responded.

I got the job.

I started in October 1987. My job was to oversee the entire flight programs for a hundred students pursuing qualifications from private to multi-engine flight instructor and helicopter ratings. The program took about forty-five weeks for each student wanting to earn an AA degree. I had a staff of twenty flight instructors and a fleet of twenty-three aircraft.

The first thing I wanted to do was make the staff look more professional. They were all working in T-shirts and jeans. I said, "I tell you what, guys. We're going to look professional. I want each one of you to go out and buy a blue shirt and get a necktie and dark pants. We're going to have a picture taken tomorrow." I knew that the way a person dresses affects the way that person acts. Dressing very casually encourages a casual attitude. Teaching flying can be done in a friendly way, but it has to be done carefully. Taking care to dress like a professional encourages careful, precise thoughts and actions.

I really enjoyed the work at Emery. It involved giving safety lectures and solving lots of aviation problems. Greeley is near the Rocky Mountains; so our instruction included the mountain flying that I knew was so important. The five-day work week left my weekends free so I could go back to Taos and enjoy my adobe home.

My contract with Emery ended in the fall of 1988. I've always loved travel and being active, and maybe I have a restless streak in me. Over the next several years, I took jobs in other parts of the country. I was a chief pilot in Indiana; Miami, Florida; and Fort Worth, Texas. In Kansas City, I worked in a cockpit resource management program for Braniff Airlines. I gave flying lessons near Dayton, Ohio, for a while. Sometimes, I taught mountain flying back in Taos. In 1985, I had been named a safety counselor by the FAA; so I was giving a lot of aviation safety talks. Wherever I've been, I've gone to work happy every day of my life. I'm a very positive person, and I love what I do. If I find myself not loving what I'm doing, I move on and do something else in flying.

I've had some interesting experiences in my different jobs. Once, when I was working as a chief pilot in Florida, an acquaintance of mine asked me for a special flight. Barbara Harris and her fiancé, John Detzel, wanted to get married two miles above Miami. I took them up to 11,000 feet in a twin-engine Seneca and circled while a minister conducted the ceremony. Apparently, the air traffic controllers were curious about why I flew such an extended holding pattern when the weather was completely clear. I just thought it was fun and sweet.

I was living in Miami when Hurricane Andrew hit in August 1992. That was a very sobering and humbling experience. It caused more than $27 billion in damage and destroyed more than 25,000 homes. It tore up airports and destroyed more than 600 airplanes where I was flying. One of those was my personal aircraft. It also destroyed the apartment where I was living. I had to move, and a pilot friend of mine invited me to move to Fort Worth and share her house.

When I got settled in Fort Worth, I went out to Northwest Regional Airport, which is about twenty miles northwest of DFW. The general aviation airport was owned by the pioneering female aviator Edna Gardner Whyte. She had been teaching people to fly since about 1930 and had trained hundreds of military pilots during World War II. She had competed in more than a hundred air races, winning more than two dozen of them. She was a fellow member of the Ninety-Nines; so I went to see her. She knew me by reputation, and she said, "Wally, would you like to be my chief pilot?"

"It would be an honor," I said. I've been working and flying out of Northwest Regional Airport ever since.

Speaking of female aviation pioneers, I had gotten my ATP (Airline Transportation Pilot) certificate in 1968, while I was living in California. That qualified me to act as pilot in command on a scheduled air carrier's aircraft. I was the fifty-eighth woman to earn the ATP. Just to give you a point of comparison, in 1970, 79 women and 34,351 men held active ATP certificates. I didn't see any reason why I couldn't get a pilot job with a regularly scheduled airline. I had the credentials and strong letters of recommendation. I applied to a couple of airlines, but was told they couldn't hire me because they didn't have women's bathrooms in their training facilities. You'd think that small problem could have been solved by putting a reversible sign on the bathroom door: "Men" on one side and "Women" on the other.

I threw it a fish and went about building my own career.

It wasn't until 1973 that Frontier hired the first female airline pilot, Emily Howell Warner. Shortly after that, American Airlines hired Bonnie Tiburzi as a pilot. That glass ceiling was broken, but not shattered. I might have been tempted to try applying again, but by then I had been promoted in the FAA as the first female SWAP (Systems Worthiness Analysis Program) specialist. I was breaking different glass ceilings.

By the mid-1980s, I was grooming one of my students, Lou Anne Gibson, for a job flying with an airline. She was one of the best students I had taught, and she knew more about engines than most women. I met Lou Anne in 1983 because her mother was a nurse who tended my mother during a hospital stay. Lou Anne's father was a military pilot, and he urged her to go for a plane ride with me. She was just finishing college and had never thought about becoming a pilot. But during our flight, I let her handle some of the controls, and she was hooked.

I put together a very intense, personalized program and took her through her private, commercial, instrument, multi-engine, and flight instructor ratings in just over eight months in California and in Taos, between mid-April 1983 and very early January 1984. She thrived on learning new skills and was a natural competitor. And she kept advancing. By late 1987, she had accomplished her multi-engine flight instructor, ATP, and instrument instructor ratings and passed the Airline Dispatchers written exam.

Of course, Lou Anne didn't land a job with an airline right away. She knew she had to pay her dues. She flew nighttime bank check runs from Albuquerque to smaller cities in New Mexico. This was in the day when cancelled paper checks were physically delivered to their home banks. She worked with me at Sierra Pacific and Emery Flight School. In 1988, she signed on as a first officer with Allegheny Air, which was owned by US Air. Her big break came in 1991, when she was hired as a flight engineer on Boeing 727s for American Airlines. She soon worked her way up to first officer (co-pilot) on 727s. She has stayed with American for more than twenty-five years.

Lou Anne is one of my biggest successes as a flight instructor. I especially like teaching young people to fly because they are eager to learn and will enjoy flying for a long time. Back in the 1970s, I had taught a young man to fly, and I was thrilled when he flew as captain with Lou Anne as his first officer for American Airlines in 2004.

Off to the Races

Teaching pilots isn't the only way I enjoy flying. I love to participate in air races. My first one was the All Women Transcontinental Air Race, popularly known as the Powder Puff Derby until the name was changed to the Air Race Classic in the late 1970s. The first time I flew in it was 1971, when the race started in Calgary, Canada, and ended in Baton Rouge, Louisiana. It was the twenty-fifth race in the series.

I flew as co-pilot in that race, with Dorothy Waltz as pilot. It was the first Transcontinental Air Race for both of us. We flew a Piper Comanche 260C. The race was scheduled to begin July 5. We flew our plane to Calgary in late June because all of the aircraft had to be impounded for five days before the start of the race. During that time they were carefully inspected to make sure they were strictly stock models. The judges would remove anything they found that wasn't part of the standard factory model. The only thing we were allowed to do to the planes was wax them to reduce the air friction.

We arrived in time to see preparations being made for the annual Calgary Stampede, but we would be gone three days before it opened. We reported to the airport runway with our airplanes at six o'clock in the morning on starting day. The first contestant took off at eight o'clock, then each of the other 149 planes took off at about thirty-second intervals. We were racing against the clock, and each team had a handicap based on their airplane manufacturer's estimate of that model's top speed. We had to reach the end point of Ryan Airport in Baton Rouge by six o'clock on the evening of July 8.

The official length of the race was 2,442 miles, but each team could plan their own route, as long as they met certain checkpoints. The race was during daylight hours only and under visual flight rules—no instrument flying was allowed. At five airports (Great Falls and Billings, Montana; Denver, Colorado; McCook, Nebraska; and St. Louis, Missouri), we had to fly by the tower at 200 feet altitude. At three other airports (Rapid City, South Dakota; Lincoln, Nebraska; and Little Rock, Arkansas), we had to actually land. All of these had to be done by the official time of sundown.

Each team had to have sponsors to finance their participation in the race. Our main sponsor was Titan Pumps, and we also got support from a company called Wigs & Hairpieces. We had to be prepared for television interviews at each stopping point. Before unfastening our seatbelts, Dorothy and I would put on the synthetic wigs our sponsor had given us. They were very attractive. We were fortunate that this was the first year participants in the Powder Puff Derby did not have to wear dresses when they flew. I was much more at home in my stylish bellbottom pants.

More than half of the teams finished the race in three days, and eight actually landed in Baton Rouge by sundown on the second day. When the scores were computed, Dorothy and I had finished in eighth place, which was good enough to earn a share of the event's $25,000 prize money. The following year, Dorothy and I placed seventh.

Starting in 1973, I added another all-woman air race to my activities. The Palms to Pines race was sponsored by Ninety-Nines chapters in Southern California to raise money to improve the air strip at Independence, Oregon. The 815-mile race started in Santa Monica and ended in Independence. My first two years in that race, I flew with Judy Campbell Broom, and we finished eighth and then seventh.

In August 1975, I flew the Palms to Pines race with Erma Orsino as my co-pilot. Our Citabria was one of the sixty-one planes that took off at 20-second intervals on a Friday morning. Later that day, we had to check in at the Merced, California, airport with either a low pass or a fuel stop. All the contestants had to land in Red Bluff, California, to spend the night. On our flight the next morning, we had to check in at the Klamath Falls, Oregon, airport and continue on to Independence.

This was the sixth year for the Palms to Pines race, and it had already generated enough money to make some improvements to the Independence airport. Its runway was being reconstructed, and the edge lighting was being upgraded. So we couldn't land there. We had to do a low pass to check in and set our finish time and then go on to land at the Salem airport.

This was also a handicapped, timed race. We finished second, two points behind the winner and seven points ahead of the third place team.

Two months later, I was flying in the Pacific Air Race with my former teammate, Judy Campbell Broom. This was a 545-mile race from Gillespie Field in El Cajon, California, to the Sonoma County airport in Santa Rosa, California. We won first place with a red-and-white Citabria.

By this time, I had developed a strategy for doing well in the air races. For months before a race, I would try out different airplanes. When I found one that I could fly 20 miles an hour faster than its handicap, I would know I wanted to use it in a race. Then, during the race, I would fly low, at about 1,000 feet, until I had to go over mountains. I was with NTSB by this time; so I was particularly conscious of safety.

I flew in lots of air races. I loved the challenge of competing against other skilled female pilots. I kept participating in the Powder Puff Derby and Palms to Pines until the early 2000s.

One race was particularly significant for me. In the 1978 Palms to Pines race, Mother was my teammate.

Little Momma and I share an air adventure

She was seventy-six years old at the time, and it was a wonderful experience for us to share. Little Momma, as I called her, wasn't a pilot; so she was in the back seat, enjoying the flight and the scenery. Nancy Brown was my co-pilot for the race. We flew a white, brown, and yellow 1977 Cessna 182. We didn't win, but we had a ball.

Once in a while, I entered races that went beyond U.S. borders. In 1982, I flew as Joyce Fester's co-pilot in the All

Women's Baja California Air Race. We placed ninth. I decided to keep going south from there and traveled on to Peru. I visited Chichén Itzá and climbed the very steep steps to the top of the 100-foot-tall pyramid.

In 1993, I flew the Great Southern Air Race through Florida and all around the Bahamas. That was a beautiful race. I placed third in a twin-engine Comanche.

Flying has been a huge part of my life, both professionally and recreationally. "Higher, faster, longer"—I have said that all of my life. I want to go higher, the highest I can go. I want to go as fast as I can go. And I want to go as long as I can go—as long as there's gas.

A Royal Presence

I have enjoyed other things, too, especially mechanical things like cars. For ten years, all of the 1970s, I showed my elegant, classic cars competitively. I started with a Bentley, but it wasn't doing well in the Concours d'Elegance shows.

In 1973, someone told me about a Rolls Royce that was for sale in Pasadena. I went to look at it and knew it was the car for me. It was a 1949 Silver Wraith, and it had actually been the Queen Mum's car in England. When King George VI had died and one of his daughters became Queen Elizabeth II of the United Kingdom, his wife, Elizabeth I, had been given the official title "Queen Mother." The car was in such pristine condition, all I had to do was put new tires on it and replace the chinchilla carpet in the back seat. Some of its mechanical features were unusual. For example, the louvers in front of the radiator opened and closed automatically as it needed more or less air flow.

This was really an elegant car. The headlight lenses were crystal, and so were the glasses and decanter in the backseat bar. The decanter was three-fourths full of liquor, and I left it there for display. Everything on the car had to be perfect for the shows. The judges would actually stick mirrors on long poles under the cars to make sure the undercarriage was spotless.

I was dating a fine young man named Michael during this time. His career was in the business world, and mine was in the sky. We had wonderful times together and cared deeply about each other. But I realized I didn't want to be tied down with a marriage. Flying was the love of my life. After eighteen months, I moved away, and our relationship just became that of good friends.

When we showed the Rolls Royce, we dressed in appropriate costumes. Michael would dress in tails and a top hat. I usually

Dressed like royalty to show the Queen Mum's car.

wore Mother's wedding dress, which was tastefully elegant. We would bring the clothes with us, but before changing we would crawl under the car to polish everything. The car was right-hand drive, and the gear shift lever was on the floor between the driver's seat and the door. I had to be careful not to catch my long dress on it when I gracefully got out of the car. One time, Mother came along and rode in the back seat dressed as the Queen Mum.

I showed the Rolls for eight years, and I won five trophies.

This was during the time I was an investigator for the NTSB. Once, when I had to visit an accident scene near my home in Hermosa Beach, I drove the Rolls. Word got back to my boss. Later, he called me into his office and said, "Wally, you don't need to take that car out to represent the NTSB."

"Yes, sir," I said, and I didn't do it again. I just loved driving it. Normally, I only drove it on weekends because I didn't want anybody to ever hit those crystal headlights. They were irreplaceable.

In 1981, NTSB sent me to London for training at the Rolls Royce aero-engine factory, and I managed to make even more of the trip. I sandwiched the two-day Rolls Royce school in the middle of a month-long journey to revisit some of the people and places I had seen on my marathon trip in the 1960s.

I flew out of LAX on a Tuesday evening in September, arrived in London the following morning, and took a train west to Pewsey, England. My friends Owen and Molly welcomed me into their home. I hadn't slept for thirty-six hours, and I was exhausted. After some delicious food and a hot bath, I had a good sleep.

The next day, I rented a VW camper and stocked up on groceries. I went to see Stonehenge, which was only a half-hour drive from Pewsey. At Avebury, another half hour or so north of Stonehenge, I found another collection of Neolithic stone pillars arranged in circles. After visiting other friends in Pewsey, I drove north a couple of hours to Gloucester. I visited Trevor, who was a flight student of mine back in 1961. He showed me the glider he was building in his workshop.

Back in London, I revisited Windsor Castle. Its rich decorations were almost overwhelming. I saw Big Ben at the Houses of Parliament and the slender Nelson's Column at the center of Trafalgar Square. Then I toured St. Paul's Cathedral.

After my typical tourist's experience of London, I drove the camper onto a ferry at Dover to cross the English Channel to Dunkirk, France. From there, I drove through Holland to Rotterdam, stopping to take a picture of a traditional Dutch windmill. The next day, I took a boat tour of Amsterdam and then shopped at the local market. Oh, that delicious Edam cheese! At the campsite that night, I paid 29 cents for access to a shower.

From Holland, I drove into Germany and spent two days in Köln. I stayed in the same campground I had parked in thirteen years earlier. It looked exactly the same as I remembered. I saw another magnificent cathedral there. Next, I went to Heidelberg and toured the fourteenth-century castle. I camped on the Nectar River in Heidelberg one night and on the Rhine River the next night on my way back to Köln.

My next stop was Bern, Switzerland, where I reconnected with my dear friends, the Hoffet family. We had a wonderful time taking the Jungfrau cog train up to "the top of Europe." Part of the trip was through a four-mile tunnel. The train station at the top was at an elevation of 11,300 feet, and the view was spectacular. While at the summit, I explored ice caves that were carved out of the glacier. Another day, I took a cable car up to the top of Stockhorn mountain.

From Switzerland, I drove down into France and visited the beautiful church in Reims. Then it was on to Calais, where I took the camper on another ferry back to Dover. Those white cliffs are always such a special sight.

After visiting other friends in London, I drove a couple of hours north and reached the Rolls Royce facility in Derby. I learned a lot about the engines they made, especially the RB 211, which was used on the Boeing 747 and the Lockheed L-1011. All that I learned there and the contacts I made during those two days would have made the trip worthwhile, but I was glad to be able to continue with more sightseeing.

I was especially excited when I arranged a tour of the Rolls Royce motor car factory in Crewe for my personal interest. I had a great day with the people there, talking about my car that had belonged to the Queen Mum. I actually met the man who made the brightwood paneling for my car's interior. He was about eighty-five years old by then. He told me, "There's a number behind each piece of brightwood in that car. If it ever gets hurt, I can replace it."

I spent a day touring Stratford-upon-Avon and Oxford on my way back to Pewsey. Another day with my friends, then back to London. This time I connected with still other friends and visited the Tower of London. Finally, I boarded a British Airways flight back to Los Angeles.

Compared with my extended journey in the 1960s, this was a short trip. I traveled 2,500 miles this time. My fuel cost $360, and the camper rental was $320. Father would have been proud of me for keeping careful records.

I've always loved traveling. During the years after I retired from NTSB, I've visited many special places. I went to New York in 1989 and stayed with a friend in Manhattan. She had been a friend of the opera singer Kay Griffel since they were children. We were Kay's guests for a performance of *Idomeneo* at the Metropolitan Opera when she appeared as Electra. We had front-row seats, and the experience was spectacular.

That was the same year I took Mother on a car trip through Illinois, visiting her favorite places and friends from her childhood. This was a sentimental journey back to where she and my father had met and married. We found the home in Olney where she was born and later married Daddy. The people who now lived in the house were very gracious in letting us look around. I had seen pictures of her coming down the curved, formal staircase for the wedding, and seeing it in person was exquisite.

In 1993, I toured California and visited lots of old friends. I even had a chance to fly a T-34 and drive a Sherman tank.

Two years later, I had a wonderful trip to Alaska. I did some bush flying and got fabulous views of the mountains and glaciers. On a fishing excursion, humpback whales and sea lions swam by the boat. I caught a twenty-pound salmon and helped bring huge King Crabs aboard.

Then I flew a seaplane to Brooks Lodge and watched bears just a few yards away catch their winter meal of salmon.

A few years after that, I signed up for a NASCAR driving experience at the Texas Motor Speedway. After some training, I drove a stock car ten laps around the track at 150 miles an hour. What fun!

THE TAOS KID

When I settled in Texas in 1992, I revived my childhood love of marksmanship by joining the Single Action Shooting Society and the Comanche Valley Vigilantes affiliate in Glen Rose. In the competitions, we had to dress in period clothing from the 1860s. I wore a white, long-sleeved, collarless dress shirt; black pants; red suspenders; cowboy boots; and a black cowboy hat with a red band

I was officially known as the Taos Kid, and that name is engraved on the handles of my pair of single-action, ivory-handled Ruger long-barrel .45 pistols. Each of them weighs about four pounds, and I had one on each hip. I also used a lever-action rifle and a short-barrel shotgun in the competitions.

Stepping back in time as the Taos Kid

The contests were fun. It wasn't just shooting at targets. Each one was acting out a scenario that might be based on a famous real incident or a movie scene. Wonderful targets would be placed at different stages, and we would have to be in a certain posture to shoot each one, whether it was prone, sitting, kneeling, or off-hand (standing up). There would be a building for us to go in and shoot, then maybe a wooden horse to mount and shoot from. We were shooting live ammo.

When it was my turn, I had to follow the storyline of that day's scenario. Maybe it was bank robbers coming to town, and I had to defend the bank. I had to study the targets and the correct sequence and postures for shooting each of them. There would be about ten targets to shoot with a pistol, about five with a rifle, and maybe two or three with a shotgun. We were judged on both accuracy and time to complete the course. I enjoyed this hobby like I did most things—wholeheartedly. I not only competed, but I progressed to judging events, too, as I did in aviation.

In 1999, I was going to judge the World Precision Flying Championship competition in New Zealand. The timing was perfect to go a little early and shoot in a black powder competition with the New Zealand Cowboy Action Shooters. I also got to fly a ski plane to Mt. Cook and have a snowball fight. And I learned more than I ever expected about sheep and sheepdogs.

In 2000, I went to Norco, California, near Riverside, for my first World Championship shooting event. That year's theme was Buffalo Bill Cody, and twelve different scenarios featured different periods of his life—the Civil War, buffalo hunting, riding for the Pony Express, and frontier living. The event lasted five days, and there were 650 contestants from the United States and several foreign countries. Besides the shooting, I was fascinated by the reenactment of Buffalo Bill's Wild West Show.

I went to shooting events all around Texas. In 2002, when I was in my early sixties, I won first in my class at the Trailhead shoot in Columbus and the Range War shoot in Fredericksburg. It was great fun, and I met many interesting people. I even participated in some Civil War reenactments and learned a lot from those.

I always liked to keep busy. Sometimes it was with hobbies, and sometimes it was extra business opportunities. Before I was hired by the FAA in Los Angeles, I was running a flying instruction operation in Santa Monica. A friend of mine, Eva Johnson, decided to open a sandwich shop near LAX. I had taught her and her husband to fly at Fort Sill, and he had been transferred to California. I went in on the restaurant as her partner. We rented a storefront and opened Eva's 101 Sandwiches. She knew how to run it, and I learned from her. People who had known me as a pilot came in and painted logos on the wall from all the different companies and scenes of me flying an airplane. The place was full all the time. People loved our sandwiches because they were really thick with meat and not too much bread. After a couple of years, Eva got sick and died. I didn't want to run the shop by myself; so I closed it.

When I moved to Taos in the 1980s, I supplemented my flight instruction business with a video company called Creative Memories. I filmed educational videos of the Taos Indian Pueblo festivals, the Hispanic fiestas in town, and all sorts of events like weddings, birthday parties, fishing trips, and flight solos. I learned to do things I hadn't known about, and it was fun.

Of course, my main business has always been teaching people to fly airplanes and do aerial acrobatics. I had quite a reputation for my acrobatic flying. In 1976, the Merrill Lynch investment company hired me to be in one of their commercials doing acrobatics in my Stearman. I did all kinds of maneuvers, including a big loop that a helicopter flew through. As I soared toward the sun, the Merrill Lynch bull was coming out of the sun, and I said, "Sure, I take risks for fun. But when it comes to my money, I'm really careful." That commercial was shown on television during the football bowl games on CBS and NBC.

Sharing my love of aviation by teaching students to fly has been one of the big joys of my life. I always stay positive and happy and give them encouragement. I want them to enjoy it as much as I do. I'm very patient with my students, calmly explaining what I want them to do as we're flying, praising them when they do it well, and suggesting ways to do it better when they don't do it quite right. I've introduced about 4,000 people to flying. I took about 3,000 of them on to get their initial pilot's license or an advanced certification or rating.

Sometimes, people tell me they would be afraid to fly an airplane. I just say, "You drive a car, don't you? More people die in car accidents than in airplane accidents." If I can get them to go flying with me, I can show them how to control the plane, and how peaceful and beautiful it is. Often, they decide they want to be a pilot after all. Mostly, I want to teach them to not be afraid of it. I will tell a beginning student, "Don't worry about losing control. I'm right here with you, and I won't let you get into trouble."

I often become friends with people I've introduced to flying. One of my dearest friendships began that way. I was getting ready to fly in a poker run at the Mesquite airport east of Dallas in the early 1990s. A woman named Mary Holsenbeck came out and told one of the organizers she would like to fly along with someone. We had never met before, but they hooked her up with me. The way a poker run works is that we had to land at five different airports. At each one, Mary would get out of my Cessna 172 and draw a card from a deck. When we got back to the original airport, we would have a poker hand. I don't remember how we placed that time, but we have been close friends ever since.

Mary had taken a few lessons from another instructor, but after that poker run, she decided she wanted to take lessons from me instead. She liked my gentle, reassuring style. Once, we were practicing stalls, and she didn't use her rudders correctly. The left wing stalled before the right one did, and we started spiraling. She panicked. She took her feet and hands off the controls and started screaming, "We're going to die!" Well, I got us all straightened out. Then she said, "Let's go back to the airport. I'm through."

I said, "Mary, I'm sorry that happened to you, but I'll bet you learned a valuable lesson. I bet you won't let that happen again, will you?"

"No," she said.

"Come on, let's do it again, and I'm going to do it with you this time," I said. I put my hand gently on hers and talked and guided her through it. Then she realized she really could control it.

After a while, she felt her personal life was falling out of control. She was going through a very nasty divorce, and one day she discovered that her husband had manipulated the settlement so she would be left destitute. She was devastated and felt that her life was effectively over. This revelation happened at a time when we had an appointment to go flying. When she didn't show up, I called her. She told me what was going on, and I said, "Come on over, and let's go flying."

"Wally, I can't afford to go flying," she said.

"I didn't ask you that," I said. "Meet me at the airport."

I knew she was emotionally numb, and I was glad she agreed. We took off, and I let her take the controls. I said, "Mary, do see that cloud up there?"

"Yes, Ma'am," she said with her soft Texas drawl.

"Point the nose of this airplane toward that cloud and just fly to it."

She told me later that flying to that cloud gave her a feeling of freedom, and a sense that there was something she could actually control. I helped her realize that she could control other things in her life, too, and that she could not only survive the divorce but move ahead and make a comfortable, productive life for herself. She has.

Chapter 8
Don't Let Your Last Flight Be Your Last Flight

The Wally Stick

You'd never believe it now, but I was quiet as a child. Maybe it was because of the way my parents expected me to behave around grownups. Mother always said, "Don't speak unless you're spoken to." I wasn't shy when playing with other kids, though. And I could get up in front of a group of people my own age, at Sunday school or camp, and give a talk.

Over the years, I have gotten used to speaking in front of large groups about topics that are important to me. When I give a talk, I am animated and enthusiastic. I rarely stand in one place, and I don't use a microphone unless absolutely necessary. I move around, gesture broadly to emphasize a point, and kid around with audiences. I love it!

I started speaking to adult groups in the early 1960s. After *Parade* and *McCall's* magazines published stories about the Mercury 13, I began getting invitations to talk about my experience with the astronaut tests. Then after my long trip to Europe, the Middle East, and Africa, I was invited to speak about that. Sometimes it was to groups of adults, and sometimes it was in schools.

By the time I was working for the FAA and NTSB, I was giving lots of lectures about aviation safety. The presentation

I've given most often is called "How to Fly and Stay Alive." I think it is important that I share what I have learned during my long career in flying instruction and accident investigation. After all the crashes I have seen, I've concluded that there are no new kinds of airplane accidents, just new people doing the same old ones.

Back in the early 1980s, two of my friends were flying in a coast-to-coast air race, and they crashed. About twenty minutes before they would have reached the end point, their propeller sheared off. Fortunately, they survived, but I started thinking. How could pilots check for propeller cracks before they took off?

That's when I invented the "Wally Stick." It's a foot-long, 3/8-inch wooden dowel. You tap it on the propeller several times, starting at the tip, where you should hear a high ping. Then as you get closer to the hub, the sound gets progressively duller. If there's a crack, you'll hear a dull thud near the tip.

Then I figured out there are other things you can do with that simple device to make preflight checks easier and more effective. One is to find out how much fuel is in the tank. A Wally Stick is marked off in inches from 1 through 7. If you stick it down into a typical private plane tank that is full of fuel, it will be wet to 7 or a little more, depending on the brand of the aircraft. I have found this technique to be easier and more reliable than trying to figure out how many gallons of fuel are in the tank. You never take off with only a few inches of fuel. You can also poke a Wally Stick up the exhaust pipe to make sure there are no dirt dauber or bird nests clogging it up. Push it against flap-track brackets to check for fatigue cracks that might be covered by paint. Tap it where the elevator and rudder weights should be, and the sound will tell you if any of them are missing.

I used to make Wally Sticks and sell them for a nominal fee

to raise money to help students who had a hard time affording to fly. Now, I encourage pilots to make their own and learn how to use them.

How to Fly and Stay Alive

That's how I start my "How to Fly and Stay Alive" talk. I go through a detailed description of how to do a thorough preflight check to make sure you are trusting your life to an airworthy plane. I use a couple dozen slides to illustrate how to do all the elements of the inspection. I tell the audience, "A safe flight is no accident, and it starts with making sure the airplane is in good condition. You don't want your last preflight to be your *last* preflight; so make it carefully."

Then I go into descriptions of about forty of the accidents I investigated for the NTSB. The photographs I show really drive home the points in my talk.

The first example is what is called a "prop strike," when the rotating propeller hits an object that makes it stop. One pilot was coming in for a landing, and he didn't have enough room for his final approach. He was probably in a hurry—that's something that contributes to a lot of crashes. He was trying to force the airplane onto the runway, but he had too much speed. The first thing I noticed when I got to the airport was a red streak going down the runway. The red cover of the rotating beacon on the belly of the plane had hit the pavement. He had come in with his landing gear up, and the plane skidded down the runway on its belly. That put the propellers too close to ground level. All three propeller blades on both engines were curled back at the tips.

My next example is from my earlier days at the FAA. A man wanted to learn to fly his Bonanza; so he hired a flight instructor. The instructor was showing him how to fly the takeoff and landing pattern at the airport. As he came in for his landing, the instructor forgot to lower the landing gear and tore up the bottom of the plane. The moral of that story is, be careful which instructor you hire. Check the instructors' records and reputations.

The next slide shows a plane that had scraped its underside during a crash landing out in the desert. It was a Mooney, a single-engine airplane with wings that come out along the bottom of the body. The pilot was doing acrobatics in it with people on the ground watching him. I like flying acrobatics, but I know that a Mooney isn't built for that kind of use. Two people died in that crash. I inspected as much of the plane as I could see, taking notes and drawing sketches. I looked into the cockpit and wrote down the readings on all the instruments and the positions of the switches. I spent about two days looking over all the parts of the plane and checking the site to see where he might have hit bushes or sand mounds on his way in. Finally, we brought in a crane and lifted up the wreckage. Then I could see that the tail of the airplane was twisted, which meant it was spinning when it hit the ground. The plane's nose was bent down, and the wings were actually pushed forward.

Here's why you shouldn't do acrobatics in a plane that's not built to do them.

Higher Faster Longer

Next up is a picture of a red-and-white Citabria that hit the ground nose first. I had flown Citabrias in races, and I liked them. They seat two people, one behind the other. It is important to be careful of the weight distribution of the occupants. In this case, a light-weight person had been in the front seat, and a much heavier person—about 300 pounds—was in the back. When they tried to take off, the plane's center of gravity wasn't within the specified range for that aircraft. The pilot couldn't control the pitch (up or down angle of the nose). The plane stalled and crashed a half mile from the runway. I don't know if it was the case in this incident, but some pilots get into trouble when they try to fly an unfamiliar aircraft. Different planes have different flight characteristics.

The next slide doesn't show an airplane—it shows a radio tower at a general aviation airport. Why? Because an airplane's elevator, a moveable part on the tail, is stuck in the top of the tower. A plane had attempted an instrument landing but was off course. It clipped the tower and ripped off the elevator. Now out of control, the plane went completely through a hangar and out the back. The plane's throttles were in the full-open position, indicating the plane was attempting to climb. Debris was strung out through the hangar, and the pilot's body had been thrown out onto the floor. It's amazing how destructive a crash can be.

Now the screen fills with a beautiful photo of the Grand Canyon. I point generally to a spot where a plane crashed. The next slide shows a narrow canyon from the ground level. It still looks like unspoiled nature. Then the view changes to what could be mistaken for a metal toy airplane smashed among rough rocks with a sledgehammer. Another view shows debris thrown away from the wreckage. Then a two-blade propeller sitting motionless on a ledge, one blade straight and the other bent toward it in a C. The propeller had been spinning when it hit the rocks.

I had been brought to that locale by helicopter but had to hike down to the crash site on foot. The river turned to the left there, but the pilot didn't. In searching the wreckage to determine the cause of the crash, I found a camera. The pictures in it would never remind the passengers of a beautiful excursion.

The airplane in the next slide doesn't look too bad. It had made a belly landing in the desert, but the fuselage (the body of the plane) was intact. No fatalities there. But a second plane at the site was a mess. It had landed on a dirt road, but I couldn't tell whether its landing gear had been down or not. The fuselage had been completely burned and was still smoldering. The first plane belonged to the DEA (Drug Enforcement Administration) and had been chasing the other plane, which was carrying a load of marijuana. When the drug carriers realized they were going to be caught, they set their cargo on fire. Some Mennonite ladies who lived nearby had come out to see what was happening. I told them, "I wouldn't stand there if I were you, because this stuff could make your mind go funny."

That wasn't the only drug case I investigated. Pilots flying marijuana in the 1970s would sit in a cabin with a load of fresh pot. Then they would crash in broad daylight on a clear runway because they were high.

The next slide in my presentation doesn't look like a crash site, at least at first glance. What is eye-catching is the appearance of the large airplane that looms behind two smaller ones. It is a modified Boeing Stratocruiser that has been enlarged enough to carry NASA's huge S-IVB rocket stage, a large satellite, or a space capsule. Nicknamed the "Pregnant Guppy," the aircraft has a nineteen-foot-diameter fuselage, and the rear section of the plane could be pulled off to allow loading of large pieces of cargo. The next slide explains why I investigated an incident with one of these planes.

In October 1977, a Pregnant Guppy landed at the Van Nuys Airport near Los Angeles. A hydraulic line on its right landing gear had broken. When the wheel touched the runway and the pilot applied the brakes, the broken line ripped a three-foot gash through a tire. The aircraft swerved and hit several parked planes, destroying one of them. There were no fatalities in this case, but the NTSB was responsible for investigating it because it was a high-profile incident. I was able to go inside the Guppy's enormous cargo bay. That was quite an experience. It was beautiful.

I show several slides of airplanes that had crashed into a hillside or onto flat ground but then struck a boulder or a tree. The force of the impact can wrap the aircraft around a solid obstruction, or it can crumple a wing so it looks like an accordion.

The force of impact crushed this wing so it looked like pleated aluminum foil.

One slide shows a small plane that came apart when attempting to land on a dirt landing strip. There is a trail of small pieces all down the runway. I had to call in a person who worked for the Piper Aircraft Company to help me identify parts on that one, because they were so mangled and distorted.

The next few slides serve as a reminder to properly maintain emergency devices. A plane had crashed in a mountainous region, and rescue teams had a hard time locating it. When I examined the scene, I found the Emergency Locator Transmitter (ELT) and wondered why it hadn't activated to send a signal that would have directed the rescuers to the scene. I opened the ELT box and saw that it was full of white, dusty corrosion. After checking the records, I found that the ELT had been manufactured on March 24, 1976, and the recommended date for replacing the batteries was February 1981. The plane had crashed in June 1977, and two of the four batteries had already leaked. Instead of the normal 12 volts, this battery pack was producing only 1.9 volts.

Just a month before, another airplane had crashed, and the ELT failed to produce a signal. The ELT had been manufactured on March 27, 1976. The battery set produced 12.5 volts; so they were still good. We tested the unit by setting the switch to the "on" or "armed" position and dropping it four feet. When it hit the ground, the switch flipped to the "off" position, and no signal was activated.

A defective or malfunctioning ELT unit can make the difference between life and death for an injured pilot or passenger. Mechanics and pilots should make sure the emergency equipment has working batteries and operates correctly.

Next, I show a plane that hit a grassy field at a steep angle. The pilot had come in too low for a landing and hit a power line. The front of the plane caught on fire, and the pilot lost control. The plane had two rows of two seats in front of the baggage compartment. After it hit the ground, the propeller traveled all the way back into the baggage compartment. That's how much force was involved.

In another crash, a plane lost power and hit the ground. At

first, I thought there might have been a problem with the fuel pump. We brought the wreckage to a hanger and examined various parts.

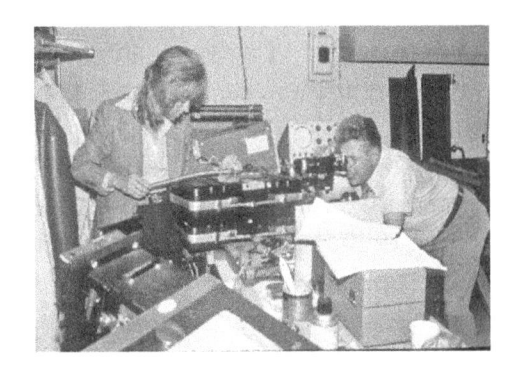

My work for the NTSB involved careful investigations like this one.

I mounted the engine on a test stand and put on an undamaged propeller. I started the engine, and it ran fine for a long time. We checked all the hoses for blockages and inspected the fuel selector valves. Then we found the problem. There was corrosion in the fuel sediment bowl. Apparently, the plane had sat unused for a long time with fuel in it, and water had gotten in and fouled the fuel screen chamber and drain port. When that material was drawn into the engine, it couldn't run.

The last picture I show is another stark illustration of the tremendous power involved in airplane crashes. A small plane had run headlong into a concrete barrier. The front half of the plane had been pushed back into the rear half. It looked as though someone had cut the aircraft in half and set the back half up against the barrier. The pilot had been despondent about family problems and had taken the plane up. He got it into a glide position, stuck his head outside the plane, and shot himself in the temple. The airplane landed itself, but then hit the wall. It was fortunate that no one on the ground was injured when this out-of-control aircraft came down.

That full presentation took an hour and a half when I gave it to pilots, and it met the requirement for the FAA pilot proficiency award program. I gave a shorter, less technical version to non-aviation audiences. I never tire of talking about how to fly safely.

I still give talks about my astronaut exams and spaceflight training experiences, too. When I speak to groups of students, I make a special effort to make my experiences relevant to them. I tell them how the upbringing my parents gave me prepared me to meet the challenges and accomplish the things I have. I encourage them to listen to their parents and thank them for their guidance and support. And I urge them, especially the girls, to become educated in STEM subjects—science, technology, engineering, and mathematics. If I had done that, I might have had a better chance of becoming a NASA astronaut.

I share with students some nuggets of wisdom that I learned from my grandfather or my parents:

- Knowledge is the power that gives us wings to soar.

- If you want to become smart, you must associate with smart people.

- To become skilled, competent, and professional, you need to be wise and know where you want to be in five or ten years.

- There are only two things you never get to do twice. You never get to make more than one first impression. And you never get to fly a jet the first time more than once.

- Don't let stress or fear into your life. You will lose faith in yourself.

- The only thing a woman needs to compete in a man's world is ability.

- Negativity contaminates energy; it slows you down. Your goal is to keep saying, "Yes, I can do it," and keep moving forward with confidence.

    I love speaking to students. They are our future. They need to hear positive messages and encouragement. They need to learn enough to be able to visualize the exciting opportunities that are available to them and how to be prepared to take advantage of those opportunities.

    In my talks to students, I talk about five A's that are important to cultivate. One is *attitude*. We need to present ourselves with a positive, respectful demeanor. One is *awareness*. Whether we're driving a car or sitting in school, we need to be aware of what is around us and what is happening. The third one is *anticipation*. Plan ahead and think about possible consequences so you will be ready to deal with them, and look to the future in anticipation of opportunities you will find. *Appearance* is very important—how you look, how you dress, and how you present yourself. This is especially important during a job interview. Finally, *acknowledgment*. People used to write thank-you notes, but that has gone out of style. Acknowledgment is still important, though. Whether it is by telling someone who has helped you or sending a written note or even an email to someone who has interviewed you, people appreciate being acknowledged, and they will remember you for it.

    I love teaching young people to fly and helping them develop the skills and confidence to be a pilot. In 1970, I had a special chance to share my aviation knowledge with students. I took over teaching the aeronautical science classes at Redondo Union High School in Southern California for a semester. I had five sections of the class. I learned later that I was the first aeronautical science teacher in twenty-three years to reach a 69 percent success rate in having my students pass the FAA private pilot and basic ground school written examinations. Enthusiasm, positive attitude, encouragement, and my own base of knowledge were the keys to my success.

A Wing Against the Sky

Ever since I was a teenager with my pilot's license, I've known I wanted to fly for a living. Aviation has been my whole life. I eat it, I live it, and I breathe it. I often say that I am married to airplanes. I've logged over 19,600 hours of flying. Naturally, I have been active in aviation organizations for a long time.

The Ninety-Nines is one of the oldest organizations for women pilots. I have been a national member since 1958 and a local chapter member wherever I've lived. Their local meetings and national conferences are always fun and interesting. They have scholarship programs for academic support as well as advanced and specialized flight training. Girl Scouts and other organizations can get educational resources from them. They have an interesting museum in Atchison, Kansas. It's the house that Amelia Earhart was born in and spent much of her childhood in. Amelia was the first president of the Ninety-Nines. They also operate the Museum of Women Pilots in Oklahoma City.

One of the activities local chapters of the Ninety-Nines do is paint airport names, compass rose symbols, and other identifying information on pavements and roofs to help pilots locate and recognize airports from the air. I remember helping paint a large "TAOS" on the runway in my home town in 1986.

The Ninety-Nines are affiliated with the National Intercollegiate Flying Association (NIFA). My Flying Aggies team won its annual air meet both years I was at Oklahoma State University. Since then, I have served as a judge at many national and regional NIFA competitions. For several years in the 2000s, the Wally Funk Competition Safety Award was given to the team that best showed its ability to maintain a safe environment while handling aircraft as well as its professionalism and behavior. Safety has been my main focus throughout my career.

Another Ninety-Nines' project was establishing the International Women's Air and Space Museum in Cleveland, Ohio. It is an interesting museum, of course, and its staff are active in organizing educational events and community service projects.

I always enjoy the annual celebration at the International Forest of Friendship in Atchison, Kansas. The Forest of Friendship was started in 1976 as a joint effort of the city and the Ninety-Nines. It is a twenty-acre arboretum featuring trees that represent all the fifty states, U.S. territories, and thirty-five countries. During the annual celebration, I am honored to carry the flag of New Mexico and place it by the piñon pine tree that represents my home state. I was inducted as one of the Forest of Friendship honorees in 1983.

The friendships I have gained through my participation in several organizations have enriched my life. It may seem like an unlikely group for me to belong to, but I always go to the All-American Girls Professional Baseball League's annual meeting. It is an organization that celebrates women who kept major league baseball alive during World War II. They showed that women, as well as men, can be good at that sport. Demonstrating the abilities of women is dear to my heart.

Another group that supports the participation of women

in traditionally male fields is the Association for Women in Aviation Maintenance (AWAM). I am a lifetime member of that organization. You don't have to be a guy to love working on airplane engines and other mechanical systems.

I also support Zonta International. It is a world-wide organization of professionals empowering women through service and advocacy. It offers three scholarship programs to help girls and women pursue education and careers in traditionally male fields. One is the Amelia Earhart Fellowship for aerospace applied sciences and engineering.

Do you see a trend here? I have lived my life in male-dominated fields, not because I had an axe to grind, but because those fields were interesting to me. I don't resent men or feel threatened by them. I just don't think there are jobs that only they can do.

Women in Aviation International is another good group. Their annual conference provides great opportunities for pilots to explore career opportunities. They sponsor an annual Girls in Aviation Day when chapters all over the world put on events to inspire young women to be interested in aviation careers. I joined the organization soon after it was founded in 1990; my membership number is twenty-six. I have spoken often at WAI conferences, and I was inducted into the organization's Pioneer Hall of Fame in 1996.

I am so fortunate to have recognition like that. In 1996, I also was the honorary race starter for an Air Race Classic event in Prescott, Arizona. The year after that, I was privileged to speak at the dedication of the Women in Military Service for America Memorial at Arlington National Cemetery. Two years after that, I judged the World Precision Flying Championship in Hamilton, New Zealand. That's just a snapshot of great experiences I had in the 1990s. Things didn't slow down after that, either.

In 2011, I was deeply honored when a Blackhawk helicopter crew presented me with an American flag they had flown during a combat mission in Afghanistan. I even had a chance to try my hand at flying that amazing helicopter at Fort Campbell, Kentucky. Then they let me do some target practice with its M-24 Bravo high-power gun. I hit the targets—what a thrill!

I have been blessed with so many wonderful honors. Delta Airlines named me to their Wall of Honor in 2017. That same year, my name was inscribed on the National Air and Space Museum's Wall of Honor in recognition of my "commitment and passion for flight." Back in 2005, I was awarded the Paul Tissandier Diploma by the Fédération Aéronautique Internationale. The citation said, "Ms. Funk epitomizes the type of perseverance, ambition, and dedication that a pilot can bring to one's life work." That is a high honor indeed.

In 2012, the VFW awarded me a Gold Medal. The citation read, "In honored recognition of her distinctive life-long career in aviation and her exuberant spirit which made her a pioneer of women. Her dedication in teaching pilots in the United States Army to fly, her many records and accomplishments and her extreme passion for aviation have justly earned her the utmost appreciation and admiration of the Veterans of Foreign Wars of the United States."

Of course, I am proud of receiving those and other awards. I am also thrilled that each of them has given me an opportunity to speak to a group I might not otherwise have been able to reach. Inspiring and educating people is more important to me than receiving accolades. I hope my message has been taken to heart.

Often, I end a speech this way: I tell the audience to close their eyes and think about what I'm going to say next. Then I read from a poem by Nancy Wood:

Wally Funk

I am but a footprint on the earth,
A wing against the sky,
A shadow over water,
A voice beneath the fire.
I am one footstep going on and on and on.

CHAPTER 9
Ninety-Nine Reasons to Travel

INDIA

When I was growing up, I was what was known as an "Anglo" in a community that was primarily Native American and Hispanic. Because of that early exposure to cultures different from my family's—along with my long trip through Europe, the Middle East, and Africa in the 1960s—I enjoy seeing the distinctive ways people in various countries express their common human identities. My participation in the Ninety-Nines has given me four wonderful opportunities for international travel.

The first was in 1977, when the newly-formed Ninety-Nines Section in India invited a group of American members to come for almost three weeks on a cultural exchange visit. They invited us to share our professional experiences with them, and we hoped to help them improve their acceptance as aviation professionals. Including some spouses and guests, 130 of us went. One of the guests was my mother. I wanted to share this adventure with her. From New York, we flew to Bombay via London on an Air India 747. It was just after midnight when we arrived in Bombay, and the tour organizers were thoughtful enough to give us the next day to rest.

The following morning, we boarded a bus for a tour of

Bombay (the city's name was changed to Mumbai in 1995). The city was a bustling, seashore metropolis. In some ways, it reminded me of Durban, South Africa, which I had visited a decade earlier. Bombay was busier and much more densely populated, though. The bus took us to Dhobi Ghat, a large outdoor area with rows of concrete basins where hundreds of people hand-washed laundry from all over the city. I had never seen anything like that before.

One of the highlights of the tour was the Mahalaxmi Temple. Thick pillars of pink stone supported a five-tiered roof over an entry plaza. A tall, square dome rose behind that. Inside were golden images of three Hindu goddesses. The Haji Ali tomb and mosque was another spectacular sight. It sat almost at water level on a rock island about a quarter of a mile out from the shore. It looked like a small, white fortress with a short dome and a tall minaret. A walkway out to it was only usable during low tide.

The next day, Wednesday, we spent the morning at a beautiful beach on the Arabian Sea. In the afternoon we visited the Bombay Flying Club. That prominent aviation school had several female students.

On Thursday, buses took us about 200 miles east to the Ellora Caves. Magnificent temples and monasteries had been hand-carved from the stone cliffs a thousand or more years before. Some were excavated inward, like caves, while others were carved as freestanding monoliths. The intricate carvings of these huge structures were amazing. They were a testimony to religious harmony, as various ones represented deities and beliefs of Hindu, Buddhist, and Jain faiths.

We spent the following day at the Ajanta Caves, about sixty-five miles northwest of the Ellora site. These Buddhist monuments had been carved into rock cliffs even earlier, around 2,000 years ago. The carvings ranged from massive pillars to life-like statues to delicate, filigree-like decorations. Some interiors featured colorful murals. It was an amazing place.

On Saturday, we returned briefly to the modern world as we boarded an airliner and flew to Jaipur. There, we were plunged back into history in the form of its ornate buildings, some the natural color of the yellow sandstone they were made of, but many painted a bright pink. The painted ones were so prevalent that Jaipur is known as the Pink City.

Sunday offered us a different kind of adventure. We drove a few miles to the deserted city of Amber, where the massive, stone Amber Fort sat on a hill overlooking Maota Lake. We were delighted to find that we didn't have to walk up the hill. We got to ride elephants! Mother and I sat together on a wooden platform on an elephant's fabric-covered back, with our driver straddling the beast's neck. We had a beautiful view from about ten feet above the ground as our elephant trudged up the hill.

No ordinary taxi for Mother and me!

That afternoon, we visited Fatehpur Sikri, a spectacular city that had been abandoned only ten years after it was built, more than 300 years earlier. It had been built quickly as a new capital for the Moghul Empire, but it had no natural source of water.

The Emperor Akbar, who had built it, relocated the capital closer to where he was trying to capture new territory for his empire. Fatehpur Sikri had been reoccupied briefly a couple of times since then, but it still seemed to be a ghost town. The massive, red limestone buildings were elaborately decorated.

We spent the following day at Agra. We saw its formidable fort made of red stone blocks, but what really impressed us was the Taj Mahal. It was elegantly beautiful. I couldn't help but think of the emperor's beloved wife to whom it was dedicated in the seventeenth century. It was one of the most serene places I have ever seen.

Tuesday, it was on to Varanasi and its dark red, stone Durga Temple that has the well-earned nickname "Monkey Temple" because of the many monkeys that congregate there. The Vishwanath Temple was a very different sight, with an onion-shaped dome between two elaborate spires, all three covered in gold. This was another city of remarkable buildings, many right on the banks of the Ganges River.

On Wednesday morning, we enjoyed an early morning boat ride on the Ganges. Later, we flew to Kathmandu, Nepal. Along with a sight-seeing tour of the city, Thursday included an airplane trip to see Mount Everest in the Himalayas. Mother and I were fortunate to get a clear view of the 29,028-foot-high peak. Some members of our group were on a later flight when fog covered the mountain.

On Friday morning, we visited the nearby city of Bhatgaon, also called Bhaktapur. The architecture there was an interesting blend of what we saw in India and what is common to China. One particularly impressive sight was the Golden Gate at Durbar Square. The entrance to a white-walled palace was set in a section of red brick wall. The doorway itself was surrounded by an ornate copper-gilded frame depicting real and mythical creatures. In an arch-shaped panel at the top of the doorway was an image of the Hindu goddess Kali with ten arms.

The city of Patan, founded in the third century, was our destination on Saturday. We saw many more incredible temples and monasteries of Buddhist and Hindu faiths. On Sunday, we had a chance to rest after so many activity-filled days. We flew to Delhi, India, in the afternoon. After a sightseeing bus tour of Old Delhi on Monday morning, we enjoyed an evening performance depicting the history of the city's Red Fort from the mid-1600s to the mid-1900s.

A bus tour of New Delhi filled Tuesday morning. The city was founded in the early 1900s; so it was more modern in appearance, although its architecture reflected India's traditions. Our tour went into some older parts of Delhi, too, where we saw monumental buildings including the tombs of Humayun and Safdarjung, two rulers who lived in the seventeenth and eighteenth centuries.

We had free time on Tuesday afternoon and Wednesday morning before boarding our flight back to New York.

That trip not only created wonderful memories, it also started a great friendship. On our first day in Bombay, I had met Saudamini Deshmukh, a member of the India Section of the Ninety-Nines. She went by the nickname of Minoo. She talked about the expense and other problems with learning to fly in India.

After we got back home, two of my Ninety-Nines friends and I invited Minoo to come to Southern California for flight instruction. I coordinated the process and tutored Minoo in ground school. Margaret Callaway gave her flying instruction in Norma Futterman's Cessna 150. Other area Ninety-Nines members pitched in to help, financially and otherwise. In six months, Minoo got not only her private pilot's license, but instrument, commercial, certificated flight instructor, certificated flight instructor (instrument), and all ground instructor ratings. She also passed a flight engineer course. She participated in the Palms to Pines Air Race in August 1977. In October, I flew with her in a Bonanza A-36 in the Pacific Air Race. We finished twenty-fourth out of fifty-six entrants.

Minoo returned to India in February 1978 and kept her skills up as a volunteer ground instructor at the Bombay Flying Club. In 1980, she was hired as a pilot by Indian Airlines. She was the second female pilot that airline had hired, and she went on to accomplish some important firsts. In 1985 she, her co-pilot, and two flight attendants became the first all-woman crew to fly a scheduled commercial flight. In 1988 Minoo became the first Indian woman to command a Boeing 737, and in 1994 she was the first Indian woman to command an Airbus A320. I'm proud of that gal.

My next international trip was a return to India in February 1986. This time, it wasn't just as a tourist. I gave a talk on aviation safety at the World Aviation Education and Safety Congress in New Delhi. After the three-day conference, I did revisit some of the places I had gone eight years earlier. In Jaipur, the Pink City, I saw some different cultural resources including a museum, the Chandra Mahal, in the City Palace compound. I also saw an eighteenth-century astronomical observatory called Jantar Mantar. Objects that looked like large sculptures were actually instruments used for celestial observations like measuring time, predicting eclipses, and tracking the locations of major stars. It was an interesting combination of beauty and science.

On the way to revisit Fatehpur Sikri, the beautiful, abandoned city, my tour group stopped and took time for a camel ride. Then we went on to Agra, where I saw the incredible Taj Mahal again.

After that brief tour, I flew to Bombay and stayed with Minoo's family. They showed me around the city. I had a wonderful time going horseback riding and giving a lecture at the historic Bombay Flying Club. Then I flew to Calcutta and stayed with Minoo, who showed me that city's sights.

I took an indirect path back to the United States because there was an airline strike going on. I had a stop in Dubai, which had the best duty-free port I'd ever seen. So many unusual items were available at attractive prices.

China

I was at home in California for a little more than a year before my next international trip. In 1987, the Ninety-Nines sent a delegation to the People's Republic of China to exchange ideas and information about aviation. Three of us were selected to speak at the various meetings we would have with Chinese groups. I would speak about aviation safety and air crash investigation. Ursula Davidson would talk about aviation education in the United States, and Sylvia Paoli would describe aviation in America with a focus on women's role in aviation.

Our group of forty-eight left on May 7, flying out of San Francisco on a Japan Airlines flight to Tokyo a little before noon. After an eleven-hour flight, we arrived about three o'clock in the afternoon. We had crossed the international dateline; so we lost a day on our calendars. To keep things simple, I just kept track of our trip as though we were still on the U.S. calendar, though. The next morning, we were on another JAL 747 that took us to Shanghai, China.

The Peace Hotel we stayed in was on the Bund, a waterfront area along the Huangpu River. That afternoon, some of us went for a walk on the broad sidewalk along the river. Many friendly people came up to talk with us and practice their English. Some of our members brought treats like candy and balloons to give the children. I had a skunk hand puppet that I operated with one hand while I cradled its body in my other arm.

Chinese children loved my skunk puppet.

Children were fascinated with it, and the adults seemed to enjoy it too. The next day was Sunday, and the riverside walkway was full of people again. My skunk was still a big hit. In the evening we had tickets for an acrobat performance.

On Monday morning, we took a boat trip along the river. In the afternoon, I went to the city zoo and watched the Giant Pandas. Traffic in Shanghai was very different from anything in the United States. In some places, the sidewalks were twice as wide as the roadway, to handle the huge crowds of pedestrians. I saw more bicycles and hand-pulled carts than cars.

Tuesday, we took a bus to the Jade Buddha Temple. The building itself was impressive, its two-tiered black roof with upturned corners topping a red wall with gold-rimmed doors and windows. Inside, the exhibits were also impressive. There were many large statues, some covered with gold. The two statues that gave the temple its name depicted Buddha and were carved from creamy-white jade. One showed Buddha sitting cross-legged in a relaxed pose. It was about six feet tall. The other was a Buddha resting on its side with one hand supporting its head. It was about three feet long. Both statues had such serene facial expressions and restful poses that I felt deeply peaceful looking at them.

After lunch, we toured a factory where workers printed designs on silk, both by hand and by machine. Then we headed for the airport and flew to Beijing.

Wednesday morning, we took a two-hour bus trip to the Great Wall. It was nice to get out of the busy city and into the quiet countryside. I found out that the top of the Great Wall is not flat. As the wall snakes up and down the hilly terrain, the sixteen-foot-wide path on top is actually a series of uneven steps. I climbed 400 of them.

We got back into the bus and drove twenty minutes to the Ming Tombs, where we ate lunch before exploring the site. The tomb we entered was underground and had vaulted ceilings. There were many beautiful items made of gold, marble, silk, and carved jade.

I could appreciate adventure in any culture.

On our way back to Beijing, we stopped at a cloisonne factory and watched people fashion the intricate designs. This technique of decorating metal objects had been practiced in China since about the fifteenth century. Artisans solder or glue delicate patterns of thin bands of gold, copper, bronze, or silver wire onto the object and also decorate it with beautiful designs in lustrous enamel. Each piece must be fired and reglazed several times to produce an even surface that is then polished to a gleaming finish. It takes a lot of patience and attention to fine detail.

We spent Thursday morning at Tiananmen Square. It is a huge, paved plaza. On one side is the mausoleum of Mao Tse Tung, where his body is on display. Then we were taken across the square to the entrance to the Forbidden City. We visited many temples filled with beautiful artifacts.

Thursday evening, we were treated to a formal banquet at the Peking Roasted Duck Restaurant. Joining us were the director of railways in China, the vice president of the University of Aviation and Aeronautics, and the director of public relations for the Chinese aviation industry. This was the first contact with our exchange partners. The meal seemed exotic to us Americans. I think the Chinese chefs used every possible part of the duck in various dishes, including the web from its feet and even its head. Quite a dining adventure!

The next morning, we took a bus to the Summer Palace in Beijing. It was a collection of gardens and palaces on the shore of a large lake. I particularly remember a covered walkway along the shore that was almost half a mile long. Its ceiling and beams had detailed scenes painted on them. It was beautiful. We ate lunch in a lovely restaurant on the palace grounds.

Another bus ride took us to the Beijing Aviation College, where we gave a presentation to the students. They asked us a lot of questions about aviation instruction and operations in the United States. How did we learn to fly? What kinds of airplanes did we fly? How was it possible to own an airplane? Were there restrictions on where we could fly? They told us about their courses at the aviation college, where their studies included meteorology, astrophysics, and aircraft design. Their English was good, except we had to explain some of our American slang.

We went to the airport for an evening flight to Xi'an, about 500 miles southwest of Beijing. After a long wait, we learned that our airplane had to land at another airport because of bad weather. About eleven o'clock, we were told the flight had been cancelled, and the airport was being closed for the night. We decided to just sleep on the waiting room benches. The airport staff provided blankets for us, and several security guards watched us from a balcony.

At 8:30 on Saturday morning, we took off in a Russian-built Tu-134. After a two-hour flight, we drove to our hotel and had lunch. We spent the afternoon visiting two local landmarks. One was the Giant Wild Goose Pagoda. Each of its seven stories was smaller than the one below it. It had been built in 704 and damaged by a large earthquake about 800 years later. Now it tilted noticeably toward the west. But it was stable, and we could go inside. The other landmark we saw was a few blocks away. The Provincial Museum was a new building of traditional design. Xi'an had been the capital of China for more than a thousand years, until about the year 900, and the exhibits were fascinating.

On Sunday morning, we had our second exchange event at the Xi'an Aircraft Company factory. It was very different from an American manufacturing plant. Everything was done by hand by people wearing no protective gear. After the tour, we were taken to a hotel and served an amazing twelve-course lunch. Then we took a two-hour bus ride to the TerraCotta Warriors site. It was stunning to see thousands of life-size statues lined up in military formation, especially knowing they were made 2,200 years ago. These were not mass produced. Every face was different.

Our dinner was another elaborate banquet. There were

twenty-six courses, each featuring a different flavor of what they called dumplings. A filling of meat or vegetables was wrapped in dough and steamed. They were tasty, but after the huge lunch we had eaten, it was overwhelming. Later, we were treated to a performance of music and dance dating back more than 1,000 years.

Monday morning, we were off to the airport for a flight to Guangzhou. We left the hotel before the restaurant opened, but they had fixed boxed meals for us. Each box had some cold meat, bread, a sweet roll, and two hardboiled eggs. I was in the mood for a little fun; so I put one of my eggs in my pocket. During our two-and-a-half-hour flight, I managed to sneak the egg into Sylvia Paoli's bag. When she discovered it later, she was surprised but caught onto the idea. She secretly slipped it into someone else's bag. That egg furtively made the rounds among our group for the rest of our trip.

We checked into our hotel in Guangzhou about noon, had lunch, and went on a bus tour of the city. Our tour of China had begun in Shanghai on the east coast, midway between the upper and lower borders of the country. We had gone north to Beijing, then arced our way southwest to Xi'an in the country's interior, then southeast to Guangzhou on the southern coast, roughly midway between the east and west extremes. We were now in the Cantonese section of China.

We had our third exchange visit on Tuesday morning at the airport, where we had a tour of the control tower and radar facilities. There was nothing surprising, because air control is pretty much the same everywhere. Then we spent the afternoon at the Guangzhou Botanical Gardens.

On Wednesday morning, May 20, we left for Hong Kong. Our three-hour train trip allowed us to see farmland and small villages. We did some sightseeing in Hong Kong before leaving about noon on Friday to fly back to San Francisco. It had been a fascinating trip. But I never did find out who ended up with the hardboiled egg.

Russia

Almost exactly a year later, I joined another Ninety-Nines exchange group for a trip to Russia. It was still part of the Soviet Union at that time. We were told that the Soviet government invited us partly because of the success of our trip to China the previous year. This would be the first women's aviation education exchange between the two countries. Our trip was actually scheduled to coincide with President Ronald Reagan's visit to Moscow for meetings with Soviet leader Mikhail Gorbachev. I was delighted to hear that the Russian hostess for our delegation would be Valentina Tereshkova, who in 1963 had been the first woman to orbit the Earth. I looked forward to keeping the promise I had made to myself in 1965: to meet her in person.

The group organizers gave us a few interesting instructions before we left. For example, we learned that taking Russian rubles into or out of the Soviet Union was considered "a most serious offence." The most we could bring home as souvenirs was the equivalent of two rubles in change. We were also advised not to bring any "unacceptable" magazines or literature such as *Playboy* or works by Aleksandr Solzhenitsyn. His three-volume work, *The Gulag Archipelago,* an exposé of the Soviet forced labor camps, had been popular reading in the United States in the 1970s. Solzhenitsyn had been imprisoned and then expelled from Russia for daring to publish such material.

On May 26, 1988, the thirty-two members of our group boarded a Finnair Airlines flight from New York's JFK Airport to Helsinki, Finland. Twenty-four hours after arriving in Helsinki, we headed back to the airport for a flight to Leningrad (its former name of St. Petersburg was restored three years after our visit). The following two days, a Saturday and Sunday, we toured major cultural sites in Leningrad. Of course, we were taken to the Hermitage. It was enormous; the magnificent art collection filled three buildings.

St. Isaac's Cathedral was also beautiful, although it did not look particularly Russian. A Greek-like temple seemed to extend out from each side of the building, with rows of columns supporting a triangle full of carved images. The center of the building was topped with a dome that looked a lot like the dome on the U.S. Capitol. The space inside was huge. Gold decorated many statues, and beautiful paintings covered the high, arched ceilings.

I thought it was sad that the glorious churches had been converted to anti-religious museums by a government that was officially atheist.

As we walked around the tourist sites, we visitors mingled with the locals as we had in China. This time, I didn't bring my skunk puppet, but the children loved the balloons I handed out to them.

That Saturday evening, we were treated to a performance of traditional dances. Red, black, and white dominated the various costumes. The music was joyful, and the movements were graceful and athletic.

On Monday morning, we had our first exchange meeting with women aviators. At each of the exchange sessions, I gave a talk about American women in space. I spoke about my Mercury 13 tests and the American women who had flown as astronauts in the space shuttle program up to that time. In just under two and a half years, eight female astronauts had served as mission specialists on flights lasting up to eight days and six hours. In fact, one of the women, Sally Ride, flew twice in that time period. Sure, it would have been nice for me to have been one of them, but I was still proud of our country for flying women in space on a regular basis.

That evening, we flew southeast to Tbilisi, a city between the Black Sea and the Caspian Sea. It was the capital of the Soviet Republic of Georgia. Our Tuesday morning tour revealed a modern city with a very long history. People had lived in the area for around 4,000 years. A river flowed through the center of the city, and mountains framed it on three sides.

In the afternoon, we had our second exchange meeting of the trip. The women pilots were interested in hearing what life was like in America, especially for women's opportunities for aviation careers. For our part, we enjoyed learning about life and flying in the Soviet Union.

The next day was a tourist's dream. We spent the morning at the Open Air Museum of Ethnography. It was nice to be able to walk around in a spacious, outdoor setting and see many different styles of traditional houses from all over Georgia. They were all built of wood. Some were plain, and others were fully decorated with intricate carvings. In the afternoon, we toured the Old City. The buildings, some made of stone and some of wood, were packed together. Upper-floor balconies added some precious space. In the evening, we enjoyed a musical play set in an earlier era.

On Friday morning, we took a three-and-a-half-hour flight north to Moscow, Russia. It was June 3, the last day of Reagan's meetings there with Gorbachev, the head of the Soviet Union's Communist Party. That meeting brought a softening in the hostility between the Cold War enemy nations, and our visit seemed to extend that feeling down to the level of individuals in the two countries.

We landed at 10:30 that morning and went directly to our exchange meeting. This is when my long-held wish came true. I met Valentina Tereshkova.

I finally fulfilled my dream of meeting the first woman in space.

It wasn't just a brief introduction, either. During the meeting, I presented her with a notebook of photos and information about my experiences with astronaut-type testing. She was only two years older than I, a couple of inches shorter, and very gracious. We sat together and had a nice conversation—through an interpreter, of course. She said she had a great time in space. She loved every bit of it, looking outside and seeing how beautiful the views were.

The next day was very special to me also, as we had a tour of the museum at Star City, the cosmonaut training facility fifteen miles east of Moscow. During our introductory meeting, I noticed the white, life-size bust of Lenin at the end of the stage. Inside the museum, the exhibits were fascinating. There was a full-scale replica of the Mir space station core module, and we could climb steps up to two wooden platforms where we could look inside the working and living compartments. We saw a Soyuz space capsule and got a good view of its control panels. Another capsule that was not in such shiny condition was the heat-scarred descent module of the Soyuz 4 spacecraft, which had accomplished the first in-orbit docking with another spaceship, Soyuz 5, in 1969. We didn't have time for lunch until 3:30, but it was worth the wait. That evening, we saw the famous Moscow circus with its skilled acrobats and performing bears.

Sunday was like any other day of the week in Russia. In the morning, we visited the Kremlin. It had not changed since I was there twenty-three years earlier. We watched the changing of the guards at Lenin's mausoleum and visited several museums. Across the Red Square, the colorful towers and onion domes of St. Basil's Cathedral were as vibrant and distinctive as ever. In the afternoon, we were on our own to shop for souvenirs.

We left Russia the next day around noon and flew to Helsinki, Finland. We spent part of the next day at the Finnish Aviation Museum. There were several biplanes that reminded me of my Stearman, and a wider variety of gliders than most aviation museums have. The day after that, we flew back to New York. I couldn't believe how much we had seen and how many personal connections we had formed in just two weeks.

Flying High

Whether it is with a group like the Ninety-Nines or just traveling by myself in the United States or abroad, I have fun wherever I go. Once when I was in Taos, I decided to land on the dirt strip at Georgia O'Keeffe's home at Ghost Ranch, near Abiquiu, New Mexico. It's about thirty miles from Taos as the Cessna flies, but seventy-five miles by car. I had to watch carefully when I landed because gophers would dig holes in the runway, and other animals might scurry across. I climbed out of the plane, walked up to the house, and knocked on the door. Remember, my folks had been friends with many of the famous local artists when I was growing up. Georgia answered the door, and I introduced myself. We talked for five or ten minutes. She was a quiet person, but we had a nice chat about the Taos art community. My parents loved her works, and it was nice to meet her. That must have been in the early 1980s.

In 1994, I spoke at an Aviation Week event on Grand Cayman Island. I made the best of that trip to the Caribbean by riding in a large sightseeing submarine to a depth of 100 feet. Then I sailed by catamaran to Stingray City, where I played with fish and tame stingrays while snorkeling. I had a different kind of water adventure on a speaking trip to San Diego once. The group that invited me took me to Sea World. When I saw the dolphin show, I said, "I've got to do that!" The Sea World people let me swim with the dolphins.

I don't know whose smile is bigger, mine or the dolphin's!

My vacations are full of adventure, too. Every fall, I go to Branson, Missouri, to see the musical shows. And every trip I also go ziplining. It's like flying without an airplane. I love it. I've gone bungee jumping, too—in Reno, Nevada, and in New Braunfels, Texas. What fun!

On one vacation, I crossed the Atlantic Ocean in two very different ways. In June 2003, I left New York on the Queen Elizabeth 2 (QE2) ocean liner and arrived in England almost a week later. The crossing took a leisurely five days and six nights. I sat at the captain's table at dinner every evening. I'm not shy about asking technical questions when I am on any sort of vehicle. The crew gave me tours of the engine room and the bridge. The engines were huge, and the bridge was very different from an airliner cockpit.

When we got to England, I spent a couple of days in London and then came back to New York on the British Airways Concorde. Half an hour before boarding started, the captain invited me into the cockpit, and the crew briefed me on what the flight would be like. It didn't look too different from a Boeing 727 cockpit, except it was more compact. After that interesting session, I took my seat. I was in the fifth row from the front of the airplane. The Concorde had a narrow body. The cabin was only about eight and a half feet wide inside, compared to the cabin of a 727, which was three feet wider. Because the plane was so narrow, there were only two seats on each side of the aisle. The front cabin could seat forty passengers, and the rear cabin seated sixty. A panel on the front of the cabin displayed information during the flight. We flew a maximum speed of Mach 2, about 1,400 miles an hour. Our maximum altitude was nearly 60,000 feet, twice as high as a 727 would cruise. The outside temperature was 81 degrees below zero Fahrenheit, but we were quite comfortable inside the aircraft. The window was only about the size of my open hand, but I was able to glimpse the curvature of the earth. That's as close as I have come to spaceflight so far.

We left London's Heathrow Airport at 10:30 in the morning and arrived at New York's JFK Airport at 9:30 that same morning, thanks to three hours of flight time and traveling through five time zones. That whole trip was such a wonderful experience. The supersonic flight contrasted dramatically with the unhurried pace of the ocean voyage. The trip was also historic. Four months later, the Concorde was retired from service. The following year, the QE2 was retired from its transatlantic journeys. I was sorry to see both retirements and considered my trip a celebration of two iconic vehicles.

Chapter 10
Detours on the Way to Space

The Space Community

I love flying. Flying is my life. My friend Mary told me she heard someone say, "Wally flies like other people breathe." That's true. I have loved every day of my aviation career, especially teaching young people to fly. And since 1961, I have never given up my quest for that ultimate flight—all the way to space.

After I completed Phases I and II of the astronaut qualification tests, I applied to NASA. They turned me down because I didn't meet their minimum qualifications, including experience as a test pilot and a jet aircraft pilot. None of us Mercury 13 did. Only military pilots could fly jets in those days, and the Navy was the first branch to let women into pilot training a dozen years later. It would be a long time before women could meet those original criteria for astronauts.

I didn't give up, though. That's not the way I am. I applied again in 1962 when NASA was recruiting for the Gemini Program. They no longer required applicants to be military test pilots. But I still didn't have the jet experience they specified.

By the time NASA recruited its fourth group of astronauts in 1964, they dropped the jet pilot requirement, but the applicants had to be scientists and then be trained to be jet pilots after they were accepted. I applied a third time, but my degree in education wasn't good enough. They told me they couldn't hire me because I didn't have an engineering degree.

"John Glenn didn't have one," I said.

They said something about him having "equivalent experience," whatever that meant.

"Okay," I said. "I'll get an engineering degree."

They gave me nine months to get that degree. No one could have done that. The time had come for me to throw it a fish. This time, it felt more like a marlin than a trout. My fourth try, a few months before I joined the FAA in 1972, wasn't any more successful. I was finished applying to NASA, but I made up my mind to find another way into space, somehow.

I guess I had made a name for myself by being persistent and by talking about my astronaut qualification exams. My first television appearance was on a national, daytime talk show. In 1973, the producers of the *Mike Douglas Show* invited me to appear in an episode. I wanted to represent my New Mexico background, which has always been so important to me. I borrowed my mother's silver and turquoise squash blossom necklace and a black leather belt with silver and turquoise conchos (medallions) to wear on the show. At that point, I was a flight instructor. We talked about my life and the astronaut-type tests I had done at the Lovelace Clinic and at other places I had arranged on my own. Mike's co-host that week was Billie Jean King. It was nice to meet another woman who was actively promoting women's rights. I knew plenty of women like that in aviation but hadn't known many in other fields.

It was another ten years after that before an American woman finally flew into space. NASA selected six women as astronauts in 1978. Sally Ride was one of them. She wasn't a pilot when she was accepted. She was a scientist. So when she took her first flight on the space shuttle in 1983, she was a mission specialist. She wasn't flying the shuttle, but she was doing experiments and helping launch satellites during the six-day mission.

I was chief pilot at the Emery Flight School in Colorado at that time. I was so excited as I watched the shuttle's liftoff on TV. Vivid memories of the testing at the Lovelace Clinic filled my mind. I imagined what Sally must be feeling as the spacecraft took off. At that moment, I wanted to be her. But mostly, I was just happy that NASA had finally flown a female astronaut.

Because I fully intended to find a path into space, I met many people in the space community. I didn't push my way in. I just went where I was invited because of my position in aviation or my experience with the astronaut testing. In 1973, when I was on my way to New York for the *Mike Douglas Show*, I met Scott Carpenter and Tiny Broadwick at a sendoff at the airport.

Me with Scott Carpenter and Tiny Broadwick, two aerospace trailblazers

Scott, one of the Mercury 7, was the second American to fly in Earth orbit back in 1962. Tiny, who was only about 5 feet tall, was the first woman to parachute from an airplane. She had been performing parachute jumps from a hot air balloon with the Broadwick acrobatic flying troupe since 1908, when she was fifteen. In 1913 she made her first jump from an airplane. She made 1,000 parachute jumps before she stopped in 1922. I really admired her.

I met Tiny again two years later when we were guests at a luncheon hosted by the Los Angeles Press Club. I met another of the original astronauts then, too. Buzz Aldrin, one of the first two people to walk on the Moon, was also one of the guests. The top of Tiny's head barely came up to Buzz's shoulder, and he was about my height. The fourth guest was Charles Willard, the fourth licensed pilot in the United States and the first pilot to carry more than one passenger on an airplane flight. I was honored to be invited as part of this group of prominent flyers.

My second visit with Scott Carpenter came in 2003 at a book signing he had for his new book, *For Spacious Skies*. Gordon Cooper, who made orbital flights in both the Mercury and Gemini Programs, was there, too. We had a short but pleasant chat about the Lovelace Clinic. I placed a photograph of the three of us in my scrapbook with the comment "Not many left from Mercury 7 and Mercury13!"

Training for Space

Even though I was finished trying to get into NASA, I never lost interest or gave up on the idea of somehow becoming an astronaut. I kept looking for testing or training opportunities. In the spring of 1991, I spent three days participating in the Space Academy in Huntsville, Alabama. It was held at the U.S. Space and Rocket Center, near Marshall Space Flight Center. It was quite an adventure and learning experience.

I was there with a group of ten men and four other women. Our ages ranged from thirty to fifty-plus. Three of us were licensed pilots, but we came from different backgrounds. There was a doctor, an engineer, a sales professional, and a writer named Sarah Rickman, who reported on our adventure. We soon found out that this wasn't going to be just playing astronaut games. We would have to learn how to work as astronauts.

The first day started with an orientation session to become familiar with the space shuttle and the training we would have. We were divided into two groups that would work together for the rest of the camp. The groups alternated using several space simulators. One was the "five degrees of freedom" chair. The chair was mounted on a stand that glided over the floor on a cushion of air; so it could move freely in the front-to-back and side-to-side directions. It also moved freely in rotating right and left (a motion called yaw), tilting up and down (pitch), and rolling sideways (roll). While sitting in this chair, I could pull myself along a practice wall and use tools as if I were working in zero gravity. When I used a wrench to tighten a bolt, my chair swung in the opposite direction just as my body would react in weightlessness on an extravehicular activity (EVA, or spacewalk). When I pushed to move higher on the wall, I just kept going higher until I stopped myself. I found out that working without gravity is tricky.

We did some more space simulation exercises the next day, too. One was a ride on the multi-axis trainer. It was like sitting at the center of a giant gyroscope while it twirled randomly on all three axes. It's a good thing I was strapped in. I knew how to keep my vision focused on the control panel as I tried to steer out of the quickly changing motions. It was fantastic. I hated to get out of the seat when my session was over. I wanted to keep going.

Next, I rode a centrifuge. That was nothing new to me, but I always enjoyed it. They only took us to 3 Gs, but it was still fun. After that, I got an idea of what it would feel like to walk on the

Moon, where the gravity is only one-sixth as great as it is on Earth. I was strapped into a harness that was suspended from the ceiling. It supported five-sixths of my weight as I walked on a sandy surface. The support was springy; so walking became a series of bounces. I suspect walking on the Moon would feel different, but the experience was still fun.

After that, each of us was assigned a role in each of two simulated space shuttle missions. We had to learn our responsibilities and practice them in the full-scale shuttle trainer.

The third day was our chance to "fly" those simulated missions. At eight o'clock that morning, my team was "launched" on the shuttle *Endeavour*. I was the commander of the space lab. I oversaw the other lab workers as they conducted their experiments and helped them if they had problems functioning in zero gravity. In the afternoon, I was assigned to Mission Control to support the shuttle *Discovery* mission. As spacecraft systems officer, I had to keep an eye on data displayed on the computer monitors to make sure the shuttle was operating correctly. On each of those missions, it was tricky trying to remember what we had to do. We had only a few hours of training for our jobs. And during the missions, the staff threw a few problems at us to see if we could handle them.

Those three days of space camp were fantastic. I was sorry to see the session end, but I was thrilled to have had the experience.

SPACE PILOT EILEEN COLLINS

About a year later, in May 1992, I met Eileen Collins, the first woman selected by NASA as an astronaut pilot instead of a mission specialist. We met at a Women in Aviation International conference in Las Vegas—the one in Nevada, not the one in my home state of New Mexico. Eileen and I hit it off immediately and became friends.

It wasn't long before Eileen got her assignment and started training to be the pilot for a shuttle *Discovery* mission. That selection actually brought most of the Mercury 13 together for the first time. In May 1994, several months before her flight was scheduled to begin, we were invited to gather in Oklahoma City, where the Ninety-Nines organization is headquartered. James Cross, a producer of aviation documentaries, wanted to interview and film us. Most of us had never met before, or even known each other's names. It took thirty-three years, but nine of us finally got to share our stories with one another. Two of the group had passed away, and two others couldn't come at that time. Eileen joined us, and we had a great time. A couple of us found out that Eileen wore the same style of watch that we did. Who would have expected that?

Ten of the Mercury 13 gathered again in November 1994. We met in Washington, D.C., to record an interview for the television show *Dateline* with Sarah James. We were sitting in front of the lunar lander exhibit in the National Air and Space Museum. Sarah asked us about the physical exams we had at the Lovelace Clinic in Albuquerque back in 1961 and why NASA hadn't allowed us to become astronauts.

The show was broadcast the following February, a week after Eileen's first launch. When I watched it, I saw that they had interviewed my old friend, Dr. Donald Kilgore from the Lovelace Clinic. He said a couple of interesting things about the women's tests:

> *We were told not to be easy on them, to give them the whole nine yards that the Mercury guys had gotten.*
>
> *What I remember is that they didn't complain as much. And the other thing that I remember is that they did at least as well as the men, and in some cases they did*

better than the men.

I was sure they were all going to be astronauts. I just couldn't believe that this extraordinary group of people would not be regarded as an incredible resource for our space program.

Eileen knew about the Mercury 13, and she invited the surviving members to attend her launch in February 1995 at Cape Canaveral. NASA treated us well when we arrived. Seven of us were able to be there. NASA took us on a tour of the Vehicle Assembly Building, that enormous structure where the space shuttle, two solid-fuel rocket boosters, and a huge fuel tank were put together before being moved out to the launch pad. They also gave us a special tour of the Orbiter Processing Facility, where the shuttle *Endeavour* was being refurbished for its next mission.

One of the great thrills of my life was watching an American spacecraft take off with a woman pilot at the controls.

At 8:30 the evening of February 2, a VIP bus picked us up at our hotel in Cocoa Beach and took us to a final briefing. Then the police escorted us to the Banana Creek Reviewing Site. We were just over three miles from the launch pad. It was chilly and dark when the vehicle launched about twenty minutes after midnight. The flames from the rocket engines were brilliantly bright. I was so excited to see a woman finally taking off to fly a spacecraft that I shouted as loud as I could, "Go, Eileen! Go for all of us!

We were still excited when we got on the bus to head back to the hotel. Our hostess said, "My bus sings 'God Bless America.'" We poured our hearts into that song. It seemed like a perfect way to end the event.

I was so pleased and proud to introduce Mother to Eileen Collins.

Eileen and I were together again about a month after her eight-day mission ended. We were both inducted into the International Hall of Fame for Pioneer Women in Aviation in St. Louis, Missouri, on March 18, 1995. I brought Mother along to share that special occasion.

I attended every one of Eileen's four space shuttle launches. She flew again as pilot of STS-84 in 1997. On that flight, she took along a pin I usually wear—a gold airplane. My pin traveled 248 miles above the Earth at 17,500 mph and covered 3.8 million miles in just over nine days. It even went into the Soviet space station Mir. I haven't been to space yet, but every day I wear that pin that has been up there.

In January of 1998, I was on a trip somewhere, and I got a phone call saying, "I think you'd better come home." The person who called didn't say why. Of course, I went to California as quickly as I could. When I got to Mother's house, a woman there told me to sit down on the couch. Then she said, "Your mother has passed away."

I said, "No way! You've got the wrong girl."

"No," she said. "Your mother has passed away."

Mother's passing at the age of ninety-five was harder for me than my father's had been because she and I had been so close and had shared so many adventures together. But I know I will see her again when it is my time pass from this life. I still talk to her every evening, and I'm sure she hears me. I tell her about what I did that day and what exciting things happened in the skies.

In 1999, Eileen became the first woman space shuttle commander for the STS-93 mission. She was commander again in 2005 on the first shuttle flight after the *Columbia* came apart as it tried to land in 2003.

That 2005 flight was special because it was the first one after NASA had made changes to the shuttles and the flight procedures to keep a disaster like the *Columbia* breakup from happening again. Eileen even had to perform the first 360-degree pitch maneuver—a full backflip—of a space shuttle before docking with the International Space Station, so astronauts aboard the station could inspect the vehicle's full heat shield for any damages.

To mark that special flight, I had arranged for an American flag to be flown over the U.S. Capitol at the time STS-114 took off. I gave her that flag when we both attended the next Women in Aviation International Conference in Nashville in March 2006.

Back in 1998, between Eileen's second and third spaceflights, there was another astronaut event that members of the Mercury 13 felt strongly about. John Glenn, at the age of seventy-seven, got his second spaceflight. One of the Mercury 7 astronauts, he had flown America's first orbital mission in 1962. Now a U.S. Senator, he convinced NASA to send him as a mission specialist aboard the shuttle *Discovery*, which Eileen had flown as pilot on her first mission. He said he thought it was scientifically important to fly an elderly person in space and compare their physical reactions to those of the younger astronauts.

Many people, including Mercury 13 members, thought Jerrie Cobb, who was sixty-seven years old then, would have been a better choice. In fact, any one of us would have jumped at the opportunity. Glenn had already been in space, but none of us had ever gotten the chance. Besides that, I felt bad for whoever the astronaut was who would have been assigned for that mission. He or she had been training and looking forward to going into space, and now their chance was being delayed so Glenn could go again. He had already had his ticker-tape parade. Did any of the women astronauts ever have a ticker-tape parade? I don't think so.

Throw it a fish.

Star City

In the year 2000, I had another near-space experience that

was fabulous. I spent a week in Star City, Russia, experiencing cosmonaut training. It was a little like the U.S. Space Academy I had attended in Huntsville, but longer and more intense. It also gave me a chance to see how Russian training and equipment compared to American versions.

I went with a group of six other trainees, four men and two women. I was the only pilot in the group. The others were a marine geophysicist, an ear-nose-and-throat (ENT) doctor, an attorney, an eighteen-year-old about to start college to study business, a toy inventor who was building his own suborbital rocket, and a journalist. Other than the journalist, who was reporting on our training, they were there as adventure tourists. It was somewhat a working adventure for me, as the Travel Channel paid my fees in return for filming my experiences for a documentary.

We arrived in Moscow on Monday, June 19, 2000. After checking in to the beautiful Radisson Slavyanskaya, we headed out to see the sights. Somehow, we made it to Red Square on the subway even though all the signs were in Russian, which none of us could read. I revisited some places I had seen on my earlier two visits to Moscow—St. Basil's Cathedral and Lenin's tomb.

After a nice dinner back at the hotel, we realized we were starting a true training experience when each of us received a glass container to collect a urine specimen for the next morning—repurposed pickle jars for the women and long-necked soft-drink bottles for the men. In fact, the next morning's first activity would be a medical checkup. We had already had a batch of blood and urine tests done back home, but I guess they wanted the most recent results.

Moscow is so far north that by the time we got ready for bed around eleven o'clock, the sun had just set. We got an early start the next morning. We didn't have to take time for breakfast because we needed to be fasting for the medical exams. A bus took us on what would become a daily ride to the Yuri Gagarin Cosmonaut Training Center in Star City, about twenty miles northeast of Moscow.

The medical exam took two hours. It included a finger-prick blood draw, an ENT exam, an EKG, a blood pressure check, and an eye exam. After a quick breakfast, we put on our personalized flight suits. The director of training gave us a formal welcome and introduced two cosmonauts who had just returned from a maintenance mission to the Mir space station a few days earlier. I would have a chance to meet them personally later in the week. The director also introduced Dennis Tito, an American engineer and businessman who was undergoing six months of training for a possible stay aboard Mir as a paying tourist.

We spent the rest of the afternoon in classroom instruction about spaceflight and our upcoming activities. A cosmonaut preparing for a space mission would have 2,500 to 3,000 hours of training. We would have thirty-six hours during our week, but it would give us at least a taste of the real experience.

Wednesday's action started with each of us taking a turn in the centrifuge. This one was larger than the one I had ridden at the University of Southern California back in the 1960s. In fact, our Russian instructors told us this was the largest one in the world, with an arm length of about sixty feet. My experience was very different, too. Instead of climbing into the gondola and strapping myself into a chair, I was strapped into a seat-like contraption so I was lying on my back. Then they wheeled me into the gondola and secured my seat for the ride. There was no instrument panel in the gondola to test my ability to follow instructions during the ride, but there was a camera so the operators could watch my reactions. I was wearing an automatic blood pressure cuff and was also wired for a continuous EKG to make sure I didn't experience any heart problems. They told me to hold a small apparatus that would trigger a shutdown of the run if I blacked out. The ride turned out to be very smooth, and I didn't have any difficulty at all. The 5 Gs they gave me felt quite comfortable.

After each of us had our turn experiencing G-forces, our group gathered to head for our next session. I noticed a young cosmonaut who was waiting for us to leave the centrifuge area so he could take his turn on the device. I knew we were here at the Cosmonaut Training Center for only a small sample of the training the real cosmonauts received, but for a moment, I felt like it was the real thing.

Next, we learned about the different types of spacesuits the cosmonauts used. One was called the Sokol survival suit. It was a pressure suit the cosmonauts wore during launch, docking, and reentry to protect them in case the spacecraft lost pressurization. The other type, called the Orlan-M suit, was used for EVAs, when the cosmonaut left the spacecraft to work outside. It was different from what I expected. It wasn't like clothing that I could put on, one piece at a time. It was all one piece, and a panel on the back opened so I could climb in.

First, I had to change from my flight suit into what looked like white long johns. I put on a leather cap that had earphones and a microphone built in. Then I started to climb into the spacesuit, putting my hands and feet into the arm and leg compartments. The instructor told me to just let myself fall into the suit. At 5 foot 8 inches, I was about as tall as the guys in our group, but I still wasn't sure how deep those leg compartments were. I didn't want to hurt myself in a tender place; so I asked the instructors to slide me gently down. Once I was inside the

Climbing inside that suit was quite an experience!

suit, I found it to be pretty comfortable.

Thursday's activity was one I had really been looking forward to. We were taken to Chkalovsky Airfield for a series of ten parabolic flight segments that would produce a total of five minutes of weightlessness. For each segment, the pilot of the Ilyushin-76 airplane would climb to 35,000 feet and then dive steeply to 15,000 feet. During that time, we would be in free fall inside the cargo bay and be essentially weightless. Thirty seconds at a time sounds really short, but it's enough time to have great fun. I had been practicing doing maneuvers in a swimming pool; so I knew what I wanted to try.

Before we boarded the plane, I was pleased to see the flight crew conduct a meticulous preflight inspection of the aircraft. Then we climbed into the spacious cargo bay. During takeoff, we wore parachutes and sat on the padded floor with our backs to the side walls. Before the first weightless segment, we took off the parachute packs and got ready for the fun. Lights flashed, bells sounded, and we floated off the floor. Twenty-five seconds later, a warning bell sounded, and a few seconds later, we were back on the floor at our normal weights. Several minutes later, we were ready for the second segment. Again this time, the instructors told us to hold on to a railing so we could get used to what weightlessness felt like. Before the third segment started, we gathered at one end of the cargo bay and held hands. We formed an ungainly collection of connected floating bodies, moving in various directions as a photographer snapped a group photo.

Floating during parabolic flight, a glorious near-space experience.

As we went through the rest of our ten segments, I tried my practiced maneuvers—rolls, pinwheels, tumbling, even flying like Superman. It felt different than what I practiced, because there was no resistance from water like there is in a swimming pool. It was an amazing feeling of freedom. I wished it would never end.

Obviously, not everyone in our group felt the same way. At one time or another, every one of the men used their barf bags.

The bags were clear, and I noticed that the substance in one of them was pink. After the flight, I asked that man what he had eaten, and he told me he had taken Pepto Bismol. I guess it wasn't designed to prevent motion sickness!

When the tenth segment ended, I didn't waste time feeling sad that the fun was over. I rushed to the cockpit, where I was welcome because of my aviation experience. I stood there for the rest of the flight, watching the four-man crew do their jobs.

The next day we explored duplicates of Russian orbiting and transport vehicles. There was a twin of the Mir space station, which had been in orbit for fourteen years. We also saw duplicates of Zarya and Unity, the first two components of the International Space Station that had been in orbit for a year and a half at that time, and the third component, Zvezda, which would be sent up in a couple more weeks. We learned about the life-support systems of the Soyuz spacecraft, which carried cosmonauts to and from the space stations.

Three of us took the three seats in the small Soyuz cabin to do a simulated docking maneuver with a space station. I picked the center seat so I could try my hand at guiding the vehicle. I found that the docking control thrusters were incredibly sensitive. It was difficult to make the fine adjustments, even with my bare hands. I couldn't imagine how the cosmonauts were able to do it while wearing pressurized spacesuit gloves.

Our final full day of training took us to the town of Korolev, where the Soviet mission control center was located. In one room, a small crew was monitoring Mir. Its official missions were over. It had been unoccupied for nearly a year, except for the just-finished maintenance mission that was preparing it for possible commercial use. In another, busier room, controllers were monitoring the first modules of the new International Space Station and preparing for the addition of the third module.

After returning to Star City, we had a short course in celestial navigation. Then we practiced identifying major constellations in the training center's planetarium. The planetarium turned out to have a unique capability. Our instructors took us into a small enclosure in the middle of the domed room and manipulated some controls. Through the room's windows, we could see the entire night sky rotate around us, much like it would if we were traveling in a spacecraft. It was very realistic.

We had a wonderful graduation ceremony when the week was over. After I received my certificate, Valery Korzun came over to speak with me. As a cosmonaut aboard Mir in 1997, he

I share a moment with cosmonaut Valery Korzun.

had helped put out a fire that threatened the space station and its six occupants. He said he thought I had done well in the training and that I should go up to Mir with him. He was wearing a uniform space pin, a small medallion suspended from a ribbon. He took it off and pinned it on me. I felt deeply honored.

All of my adult life, I have followed the progress of human spaceflight and participated in as many related activities as I could. Today, in my living room, I have two television sets. One is always on, tuned to the NASA channel so I can see what is going on in the International Space Station and learn about other space activities and events.

In 2006, Anousheh Ansari flew as a private citizen to the International Space Station. She was the fourth person, and the first woman, to purchase a flight as a space tourist. I had met her two years earlier at the conclusion of the Ansari X-Prize competition she had helped finance, and I had been following her blog as she prepared for her trip. The day before she launched, she wrote, "It is hard to explain my feelings … a strange mix of excitement and anxiety.… I just want to get the launch behind me and start floating in the wonderful weightlessness of space."

I posted the following comment in reply:

Dear Anousheh,

I am so very proud that you're fulfilling a dream that we both share. My dream has continued for 46 years after the Mercury 13 testing and additional testing in Star City 2000. My heart flies with you and wishing you all the very best.…

Looking forward to your comment and return. You're doing a wonderful thing to encourage the youth of today to continue their math and science. Anything is possible.

Looking forward to hearing from you while you're looking down on us. When you fly over Texas just know I will be looking up and smiling.

Wally

In 2017, I was invited to travel to England, France, and Germany to record a BBC radio documentary called "The First

Woman on the Moon." I visited the European Space Agency (ESA) Astronaut Training Centre in Cologne and met Italian astronaut Samantha Cristoforetti. I spoke with ESA's director general, Jan Woerner. And I had a close-up view of a full-scale model of the ExoMars rover in a sand room that is designed to imitate the surface of Mars.

I have had the pleasure of doing many things related to space travel. I've trained, practiced, met experienced people, and seen and learned many things. It has all been wonderful, interesting, and fun. But I still want the real thing.

CHAPTER 11
She's Got a Ticket to Fly

SPACE ADVENTURES

The teaser for the Travel Channel's documentary about my experiences at the Yuri Gagarin Cosmonaut Training Center in Russia opened with a video of me bouncing around weightlessly during one of the parabolic flight segments. The narrator said, "Who pays $20,000 to be kicked around on vacation? She does."

Well, the other people in my group at Star City in 2000 may have thought of the week as a vacation or a special one-time adventure, but I was serious about it. I was still working on getting myself into space. In 1997, I had signed on with Zegrahm Voyages, a company that was offering suborbital spaceflights for paying customers. The training I had at Star City was preparation for that spaceflight.

In late 1999, Space Adventures bought Zegrahm, but the details of the spaceflight stayed the same. The vehicle was going to be a two-stage affair developed by Vela Technology Development. A mothership called the Sky Lifter would take off from an airport and carry the spaceship, called the Space Cruiser, for the first leg of the flight. Sky Lifter was a beautiful delta-wing airplane powered by two turbo-jet engines. It carried Space Cruiser under its belly.

The paired vehicles would take an hour and twenty minutes

to reach 50,000 feet, and then the spacecraft would drop away and ignite its three rocket engines that used nitrous oxide and propane as propellants. Those engines would fire for two minutes, pushing the vehicle to an altitude of forty miles. The spaceship designers figured the acceleration would produce only 2 Gs of force. After shutdown, the Space Cruiser would coast to an altitude of sixty-two miles, which is a commonly accepted definition of reaching space. The six passengers and two pilots would experience two and a half minutes of weightlessness and views of the Earth.

As the ship was falling back down, the pilots would use its rocket retroengines to help slow the descent, again producing only 2 Gs of deceleration force. A few minutes later, at an altitude of 70,000 feet, they would shut off the retrorockets. After another ten minutes, the craft would be at an aircraft cruise altitude of 30,000 to 40,000 feet and would fly like an airplane, using two turbo-jet engines, back to the airport runway. The entire trip would take about two and a half hours. It all sounded great.

The Space Cruiser System was still in development, and the first test flight was expected in late 2001. So, this exercise in Star City was very timely. Actual passenger-carrying flights were expected to start in 2003. The passengers' space suits had been designed, and instructors were training to help customers with a week of preparation just before their flights. I wasn't the only one who believed in this opportunity. At least seventy-five customers had signed up. The Dole food company ran a contest that offered a ticket for the trip as first prize.

A few years went by, and the flights never happened.

Throw it a fish.

WALLY'S TICKET TO SPACE

By early 2002, I had another opportunity that was even more

exciting. It came from Randa and Rod Milliron, the owners of Interorbital Systems. They were designing a different type of spacecraft, one that was more like the ones used by NASA and the Soviet Union. The *Neptune* Spaceliner would be a two-stage, vertical-takeoff rocket that would carry four passengers and two pilots to an altitude of 150 miles for a weeklong stay in Earth orbit. That's what I'd been waiting for. Seven days in space would be my dream come true.

Randa and Rod explained all the details to me during many phone conversations. They said the passengers would experience up to 5 Gs during the eight-minute launch phase. Once the ship was in orbit at 17,370 miles an hour, the pilots would reconfigure the vehicle to provide access to a Habitable Orbiter Stage with plenty of room and windows. The crowning touch of the experience would be that each passenger would spend time outside the spacecraft on a spacewalk, safely tethered to the vehicle and attended by one of the pilots.

It got even more unusual than that. The flights would be launched from a new spaceport they were working on developing in the South Pacific. There would be a training facility on an island of Tonga, about 2,000 miles northeast of Australia's east-coast city of Brisbane. The actual launch would take place with the *Neptune* partially submerged in the ocean. How exotic is that!

Even before I contacted them for information about their plans, the Millirons had been doing research on my flying experience and my efforts to get into space. They wanted me to fly first as a passenger, and then to train to be a permanent member of the astronaut pilot crew.

"You are the most qualified person in the world for this," Randa told me. "We want someone who can think on her feet."

I was certainly intrigued. I had wanted to be an astronaut for 41 years by then, and I wanted to seize any realistic opportunity.

"You should have been the first woman in space," Randa told me. "We would like for you to join us."

I asked a lot of questions about what they were doing. I found out they had already built and tested rocket components. They had even built a small single-stage rocket as a technology demonstrator.

Finally I said, "I'm your girl. Sign me up."

The Millirons' ambitious plans for orbital tourism flights still had a long way to go before tests could start. My being a part of the Interorbital team at an early stage would give Interorbital publicity and might help them raise money for their developments. Paul Harvey, the legendary radio personality, even announced it on his national news and commentary broadcast. The Millirons promoted a campaign to finance the cost of my orbital trip by soliciting different levels of sponsorship. They called it "Four Ways You Can Buy Wally's Ticket to Space." For amounts ranging from $2 million to $5 million, investors could not only buy my ticket but make a contribution to the Trans Lunar Research nonprofit organization, fund an advertising campaign, or buy an equity stake in Interorbital Systems.

Another financial opportunity was available at that time, too. It was called the Ansari X Prize, with a $10 million dollar top award that was largely financed by Anousheh Ansari and her brother-in-law, Amir Ansari. The purpose of the contest was to encourage the development of a spacecraft without government funding that could carry a pilot and two passengers on a suborbital flight to space and repeat the flight using the same vehicle within two weeks. The Millirons decided to enter that competition, even though it was only for suborbital flights. Winning the huge prize would help them finance their orbital program.

I then became the official test pilot for their entry in the suborbital contest. The vehicle they entered, called the Solaris

X, would eventually be the orbital stage of the Neptune launch system. The Interorbital Systems company operated from a hangar at the Mojave Airport in Southern California. I went there in 2003 to watch the static test firing of their rocket engine. Seeing and hearing that exhaust blast was thrilling. I also climbed into the housing for the flight capsule. This was all beginning to feel real.

Ron Milliron was the more technical part of the Interorbital team. He had previously worked for Grumman Aerospace and General Dynamics. Randa helped with hardware development and testing, but she was also in charge of promotion and marketing. She knew that pulling together a high-profile team could help attract sponsors. About the same time she brought me on board, she announced that Chalmers "Slick" Goodlin had joined the Interorbital Systems Advisory Board. He had been the first test pilot to fly the experimental Bell X-1 plane under its own power. Slick would help develop the company's pilot training program.

The next year, Randa came up with another promotional idea. She enlisted seventeen-year-old Justin Houchin to train as my co-pilot. A teenage rocket pilot was sure to attract attention. He wasn't even a licensed airplane pilot yet, but I could help with that.

Justin arrived at my home base of Northwest Regional Airport in Roanoke, Texas, in the fall of 2003. I knew he had already taken some flying lessons. We did our preflight inspection, got settled in our seats, and I taxied out to the runway. I guess he was surprised when I said, "Go ahead and take off." I figured he had come to fly; so I was going to let him.

I could tell he was nervous. But I just talked to him very calmly, and he started to relax a little. He took off just fine. I talked him through some maneuvers in the air and guided him through communications with the tower. After a while, I told him to go ahead and land. He seemed a little surprised again, but he was getting to be pretty comfortable with me. He landed smoothly. He already knew what he was doing, and I just gave him some more confidence in his ability to fly.

Justin later said, "I did more with Wally on that one day than ten days of my formal flying lessons." He loved it.

A few months later, Randa arranged for Justin to get two days of training at the National Test Pilot School in Mojave. The first day was all instruction. On the second day, he strapped into therear seat of an Aermacchi Atlas Impala jet trainer with an experienced flight instructor in the front seat. They flew for forty-five minutes doing banks, rolls, and loops. Several times, the pilot let Justin take the controls for a few minutes, even guiding him to perform some rolls. The kid was talented and an attentive student. I love seeing young people accomplish their dreams and gain self-assurance. I was happy to think he would fly with me for Interorbital.

We were hoping to make our first attempt at the Ansari X Prize in late 2004, but another team was ready to fly before our rocket was complete. That was the Scaled Composites group led by Burt Rutan. They won the competition that October. A mothership called WhiteKnightOne carried their SpaceShipOne vehicle on a flight profile much like the one the Space Cruiser System had planned to do. The most visible difference was the design of the mothership. Sky Lifter had been a sleek airplane, but WhiteKnightOne was two airplane fuselages joined together by a common wing. The spaceship was attached to the middle of that common wing. It was an impressive sight.

The spaceship released from the mothership at about 50,000 feet and powered itself above the required 62-mile altitude. It carried one pilot and ballast to represent the weight of two passengers. The spaceship glided back in for an unpowered landing on the same runway the mothership had taken off from. The team was able to get the same two vehicles ready for their second successful flight only five days later to claim the prize.

I watched their winning flights on September 29 and October 4 as an invited guest. They were spectacular. I was also invited to the award dinner in St. Louis later that year. During those times, I heard of a person named Sir Richard Branson. He was a Brit who contracted with Burt Rutan to develop larger versions of the vehicles that won the Ansari X Prize. Sir Richard's new company, Virgin Galactic, would use them for space tourism flights.

Virgin Galactic

The Interorbital team was still working on their orbital rocket, but they never completed a person-rated spacecraft. They're still in business, making rockets for launching small satellites. They were even part of a team that competed for the Google Lunar X Prize competition that ended in 2017.

But by 2010, I could see that a more promising opportunity to get myself into space was coming along. Some travel agents who were authorized to sell tickets for Virgin Galactic's suborbital flights contacted me. The flight they described sounded really familiar. I almost felt like I had gone back to 1997 and was talking with the folks from Zegrahm again. But some things were clearly different.

Virgin Galactic was making good progress toward starting their space tourism flights. They had actually built one of their new motherships, a WhiteKnightTwo aircraft named *Eve*, and a SpaceShipTwo craft named *Enterprise*. The spaceship's systems were being ground tested, and its first unpowered flight test was coming up in a few months. More than that, they had reached an agreement with my home state of New Mexico to build a spaceport that they could use for their horizontal takeoff and landing flights. The spaceport was being built next to White Sands Missile Range so its restricted airspace would keep private and commercial airplanes away from Virgin Galactic's launch and landing activities.

I had hoped to get to space on the Space Cruiser or Interorbital's Solaris X or Nautilus, but I have also been realistic. All along, I've said that I won't believe it until I'm on the rocket and the engines start. Still, Virgin Galactic was clearly moving ahead and making progress. Maybe this time it could happen.

On July 1, 2010, I took the plunge. I wrote a $200,000 check to Virgin Galactic for the full ticket price. I'm not a wealthy person, and I invested my life savings in this opportunity. If it would finally take me to space, it would be worth it.

Soon after I signed up, Virgin Galactic sent me a beautiful model of the spaceship attached to the mothership. Sir Richard treats his ticket holders well. That's good, because the Virgin Galactic flights have been delayed over and over. When I bought my ticket, they expected to start carrying passengers by 2012. Now, we'll be lucky if I get my ride in 2021.

The company keeps us feeling involved by offering special events once or twice a year. Sometimes they are at the vehicles' construction and testing facility in Mojave, and other times they are at Spaceport America in southern New Mexico, where the flights will actually happen.

The first event I went to was the ceremony to dedicate the Spaceport America runway in October 2010. The location was beautiful—a wide, flat expanse with low mountains on the horizon. Wispy clouds set off the deep-blue New Mexico sky. The main spaceport building was still under construction. In the future, it would house the astronaut training facility, the flight operations center, and the hangar for the Virgin Galactic fleet. Hundreds of people were wandering around when Sir

Richard arrived aboard a private jet that landed on the beautiful new runway.

New Mexico Governor Bill Richardson hosted a nice ceremony. Several people spoke as we sat on folding chairs on the taxiway between the hangar and the runway. As Sir Richard was finishing his speech, the mothership carrying the spaceship flew overhead. It was quite a sight. The huge, combination vehicle circled around and overflew the crowd several times. Watching it appear over the partially-built main structure and fly low over us was thrilling.

I am openly excited about going into space. I remember that when the joined vehicles flew above us, I let out a yell. It felt like I was really going to make it to space after all the years of trying.

Finally, it landed on the runway and parked at the edge of the taxiway. We weren't allowed to go all the way up to it, but we were pretty close. Before the festivities ended, I had my picture taken with the governor, Sir Richard, and former astronaut Buzz Aldrin.

Before I went home, I got permission to fly over the spaceport. I wanted a birds-eye view. I didn't have permission to land on the restricted runway, but I snapped a good aerial photo of it. I wondered how different it will feel to be aboard SpaceShipTwo when it comes back from a suborbital flight and glides to a silent, unpowered landing on that strip.

About a year later, I was back at the spaceport for another ceremony. This was a dedication of the terminal and hangar building. A large crowd had gathered again, and now the building looked spectacular. A three-story wall of glass looked east toward the runway, which ran north and south. As usual, Sir Richard made a dramatic entrance. He rappelled down that glass face, along with a troop of acrobatic dancers. Then he spoke about the flights that would eventually use this spaceport. With his usual excitement, he said he still expected to start commercial operations by the end of 2012. At the reception following the speeches, I was introduced to Sir Richard's mother and had a nice chat with her. She reminded me of my Little Momma.

In September 2013, I went to a ticket-holder gathering in Mojave. That time, I was able to go right up to the spaceship in the hangar and put my hands on her hull. It had been named after the starship *Enterprise* in *Star Trek*. This wasn't a mockup, but a functional vehicle. It had already flown up to 56,000 feet in a test flight and showed promise of working its way up to full altitude in future tests.

On Halloween Day 2014, I was stunned to hear that the *Enterprise* had crashed during a test flight. The pilot bailed out and was injured, but the co-pilot died in the crash. What would this mean for the company's future? If the design was faulty, it could take years to re-engineer it. Nine months later, the NTSB released the results of its investigation of the crash. Like so many of the crashes I had investigated decades before, the primary cause was found to be human error. The spaceship was designed so the crew would raise its twin tail booms to slow and stabilize the craft during its unpowered descent from space. In this flight, though, the co-pilot had mistakenly activated that braking system while the spaceship was ascending under full power. It tore the vehicle apart. The vehicle designers had to devise a way to keep the braking system from being activated until the unpowered descent phase of the flight. They also made other safety improvements to the vehicle's design and the pilot training programs.

It was tragic that human error had cost a life and destroyed a valuable spacecraft. But I was relieved that the crash hadn't been caused by some fundamental design flaw.

Virgin Galactic had started building a second SpaceShipTwo in 2012. This was a hand-built vehicle, not a mass-production model. It wasn't completed until February 2016. I attended a ticket-holder gathering in Mojave when the new spacecraft, named *Unity*, was unveiled. There were months of flight testing still ahead.

In September 2017, a group of ticket holders gathered again at Spaceport America.

Spaceport America, the place where I'll finally take off for space.

This time, it was a small gathering, just seven ticket holders along with their guests. We stayed in a nice hotel in Las Cruces, New Mexico, and were driven the forty-five miles out to the spaceport in luxurious Land Rovers. Our drivers took us out onto the 12,000-foot-long, 200-foot-wide runway, and we raced side by side in a thrilling ride. Then we had a chance to explore the nearly finished interior of Virgin Galactic's terminal and hangar areas. They were beautiful.

At sunset, we gathered in the hangar for a spectacular banquet that was prepared on site. The huge space, large enough to house two motherships and five spaceships, held only a full-scale mockup of SpaceShipTwo. Fifteen of us were seated around a black-clothed, rectangular table littered with blue-beaded centerpieces, tall pitchers of ice water, and stemmed glasses of chilled white wine. The chef created an amazing meal with flaky-crusted hot appetizers, crisply steamed vegetables, tender meat, and an out-of-this-world dessert nestled in dry-ice vapors. After dark, we had a chance to walk outside and see the beautiful terminal building lit from within.

The next day, back in Las Cruces, we joined a group of middle-school students for a simulated space mission at the Challenger Learning Center. Each of us participated right along with the youngsters. What fun it was to see them take on their assigned roles and perform their duties, either in mission control or aboard a space shuttle. It is so important that we instill in students the value of studying science, technology, engineering, and math.

It wasn't until the following April, in 2018, that *Unity* made its first powered test flight. The date of my trip into space kept slipping and slipping.

This Kid Has No Regrets

I have firmly believed—no, more than that—I have *known* since 1961 that I would one day fly into space. The date of my trip into space still hasn't been announced. Somehow, sometime, it will happen.

Whether it was the way I was brought up or just my personal nature, I have always been a positive person. I have enjoyed every moment of my life. When things haven't worked out the way I would have liked, my philosophy has always been to get over it and move on. I haven't changed.

Because of my quest for spaceflight as well as my aviation career, I have been invited to speak at interesting places all over the world. One place that has become very special to me is right here in the United States. The Portal of the Folded Wings is a beautiful, dome-covered building with four arched entryways at the Valhalla Cemetery in Burbank, California. It is a shrine to "the honored dead of American Aviation," and the ashes of more than a dozen aviation pioneers are interred under the floor of the structure. In 2007, a 21-foot-long replica of a space shuttle was installed in front of the portal as a memorial to the astronauts who died in the *Challenger* and *Columbia* disasters. It was an honor for me to speak at the dedication of that memorial.

Bobbi Trout is one of the aviation pioneers whose ashes are buried in the portal. She set several aviation records back in the 1920s and 1930s. In later years, she became a dear friend and mentor to me. She died in 2003 at the age of 97. I have reserved a space for my ashes to be buried next to Bobbi's when it is my time to go.

I don't get emotional about passing from this life. I have faith that I will join my dear mother, my father, and my many friends who have gone before me when it is my turn to go. I have had a wonderful life filled with amazing experiences.

I have been preparing for my flight into space since 1960. Striving for that goal has already made my life more interesting, more exciting than it would have been otherwise. Because of that goal, my fascination with aviation, and my travels and hobbies, I have made many great friends.

This kid has no regrets.

God bless you all.

Wally Funk

*I salute all space travelers and have
done my best to join you.*

TO THE READER
Notes for Context

CHAPTER 1

Around a thousand years ago, peaceful Native American groups began to build villages in what is now the American Southwest. Their buildings were commonly made of local clay and water. The buildings were clustered together, like modern apartment complexes, with the upper stories terraced back from the lower ones. After the arrival of Spanish colonizers at the end of the sixteenth century, these Indian settlements became known as "pueblos," the Spanish word for "villages." The Pueblo Indians developed agriculture as well as hunting for their food sources.

Taos Pueblo is one of nineteen pueblos in New Mexico that are still inhabited. It is unusual in that the larger of its two main adobe buildings is five stories tall.

The current population of the town of Taos, two miles from Taos Pueblo, is about 4,500. During Wally's childhood, the population was around 1,500.

The area began attracting Anglo artists in the mid-nineteenth century, and a group formally founded the Taos Society of Artists in 1915. That organization lasted only until 1927, but the artists and authors kept coming. During Wally's childhood, Taos and its surrounding areas were home to such notables as Mabel Dodge Luhan, Georgia O'Keeffe, Ernest Blumenschein, Ansel Adams, and D.H. Lawrence. The first book featuring Ansel Adams' photographs, *Taos Pueblo*, was published in 1930.

That was the same year that a pioneer of a different type moved to New Mexico. Dr. Robert H. Goddard, a physics professor from Massachusetts, moved to Roswell in the southeastern corner of the state to continue his research. In pursuit of his lifelong quest of furthering the ability of humans to travel beyond the Earth, he had invented the liquid-fuel rocket in the previous decade. It was the fundamental step toward the spaceflight that Wally sought throughout her life. She was born in 1939, two years after his highest test launch, which reached an altitude of well over a mile and a half. Wally was unaware of Goddard's research during her childhood. New Mexico is a large, primarily rural state, and Roswell is more than 250 miles from Taos.

Chapter 2

The "space race" was a Cold War battle between the Soviet Union and the United States, with the objective of proving whether a communist form of government or a democracy was superior. The Soviet Union fired the first salvo in October 1957 with the launch of Sputnik I, the first artificial satellite.

About the time Wally was beginning her junior year at Oklahoma State University in the fall of 1958, NASA (the National Aeronautics and Space Administration) was beginning to function. It absorbed a Man in Space Soonest program the U.S. Air Force had started earlier that year. With this change, America's efforts to put humans in space before the Soviet Union became a civilian function rather than a military one. NASA named its initial manned space program Mercury and began planning to select its first astronauts.

Chapter 3

NASA formed a team of aeromedical experts from the armed services and an independent civilian Life Sciences Advisory Committee to help define the astronaut selection process. The head of the Life Sciences Advisory Committee was Dr. William Randolph (Randy) Lovelace II of Albuquerque, New Mexico. His clinic had been conducting secret physical examinations of military pilots for clandestine, very high altitude U-2 flights since 1956. The Lovelace Clinic was selected to design and conduct the physical examinations of the Mercury astronauts in early 1959.

President Dwight Eisenhower had decided that America's astronaut candidates would be drawn from the pool of military test pilots. This ensured that the candidates would be accustomed to dealing with emergencies under stressful conditions and would be familiar with the physical and psychological stresses of high-speed flight in unproven aircraft. Furthermore, they would already hold security clearances. Candidates had to be less than forty years old, less than five feet eleven inches tall, and have at least 1,500 hours of flying time, much of it in jet aircraft. The initial phase of the selection process identified 110 potential candidates.

A first round of screening produced thirty-two men who met the basic qualifications and were interested in participating. They were sent to the Lovelace Clinic in Albuquerque for physical examinations. They arrived in groups of six at a time, with each group being tested for seven and a half days. Only one of the thirty-two was disqualified for medical reasons.

The Master's Two-Step test consisted of the subject stepping up and back down a two-step platform for ninety seconds at a specified rate determined by the subject's weight and age. Each step was twelve and a half inches tall. The subject's blood pressure and heart rate were measured before the stepping activity and again two minutes afterward to evaluate the subject's tolerance to exercise.

The Mercury astronaut candidate physical examinations were extraordinarily thorough. The physical effects of spaceflight on humans were unknown; so the examinations measured every conceivable physical characteristic. The data would also provide a set of baseline measurements for each astronaut that could be compared to post-spaceflight data in order to identify any physical effects caused by exposure to microgravity and cosmic radiation. By the time the next astronaut candidates were tested for the Gemini program in 1962, their greatly simplified physical exam took only one day.

Except for Jerrie Cobb, who had taken the physical exams at the Lovelace Clinic in 1960, Wally and the other women had their exams in 1961. NASA's manned space program was not the only prominent news in the United States that year. Civil rights demonstrations were under way in the South, and violence broke out at such events as the court-ordered desegregation of the University of Georgia. Feminism was on the rise, and in late 1961 President John Kennedy established the President's Commission on the Status of Women, chaired by former First Lady Eleanor Roosevelt. Among other things, the Commission found that women in the workplace earned only 59 percent of what their male counterparts did. This was a time when women's legal rights were limited, including being able to get a credit card unless she had a husband who was willing to cosign for it.

Chapter 4

The thirty-one male astronaut candidates who passed the Lovelace Clinic medical examinations then spent a week at the

Aeromedical Laboratory at Wright Air Development Center in Ohio, undergoing psychological examinations and physical stress tests. At the end of that time, eighteen men remained viable candidates. A screening committee reviewed their data and selected seven to become Mercury astronauts. They were Scott Carpenter, Gordon Cooper, John Glenn, Gus Grissom, Wally Schirra, Alan Shepard, and Deke Slayton.

NASA authorized and funded the examinations of the male Mercury astronaut candidates. When Dr. Lovelace decided to conduct the same physical examinations on highly qualified female pilots, he was acting without the knowledge or consent of NASA. It was a research project funded largely by Jackie Cochran and her husband, Floyd Odlum. Lovelace hoped that the results would be compelling enough for NASA to consider the women as potential candidates. In his optimism, he gave the women test subjects a stronger implication of their chances than was justified. When he attempted to proceed with testing some of them at the Pensacola Naval Air Station in Florida, NASA became aware of the request and declined to authorize the use of the facility.

The Mercury 13 could be forgiven for assuming their testing would lead to their acceptance as astronauts. For example, a syndicated columnist who interviewed Dr. Lovelace wrote in September 1960 that "He expects to have all twelve of the female astronauts picked by next January." In a *Dateline* interview taped in 1994, Jerri Truhill said, "Even the people in the [Lovelace] clinic would say, 'Gee, I envy you. You're going to get to go into space.'"

As Wally has mentioned in Chapter 4, Jerrie Cobb and Janey Hart testified before a Congressional committee that was looking into whether the astronaut selection process was biased against women. (Sex discrimination did not actually become illegal until passage of the 1964 Civil Rights Act.) Jackie Cochran testified at the hearing, and members of the Mercury 13 were surprised at her lack of support for their cause. In part, she said, "Because very few individuals will be used as astronauts in the near future and there is no shortage of well-trained and long-experienced male pilots to serve as astronauts, it follows that present use of women ... cannot be based on present need." She also commented that it is expensive to train an astronaut and that such an investment would be wasted if a trained woman decided to get married and/or start a family.

Mercury astronauts John Glenn and Scott Carpenter also testified. Although they generally reflected attitudes about gender roles of that era, some of the comments sound strange in today's society. For example, Glenn said, "The men go off and fight the wars and fly the airplanes and come back and help design and build and test them. The fact that women are not in this field is a fact of our social order." He did concede that "It may be undesirable."

Some innuendos reflected similar, now outdated, attitudes. At one point, Representative James Fulton of Pennsylvania asked Glenn, "Why wouldn't a woman be good company on a trip to the moon?"

Glenn's response, "... if we can find any women that demonstrate that they have better qualifications for going into a program than we have going into that program, we would welcome them with open arms," was greeted with laughter. Then Glenn jokingly said, "For the purposes of my going home this afternoon, I think that should be stricken from the record."

Chapter 5

Wally's visit to Moscow was almost a year and a half after Valentina Tereshkova flew a three-day solo mission in Earth orbit for the Soviet Union. When Wally tried to arrange a meeting with her, Valentina's baby daughter was about five months old. Valentina had married fellow cosmonaut Andriyan Nikolayev in a high-profile wedding that was encouraged by authorities of the Soviet Union's space program. The marriage was not successful.

Wally's extended trip through Africa in 1966 and 1967 came at an interesting time politically. Egypt and South Africa had long histories of self-government, having been independent since 1922 and 1910, respectively. Morocco had also been independent for a decade. On the other hand, Angola and Mozambique would remain colonies of Portugal until 1975, and Rhodesia (later Zimbabwe) would remain under British rule until 1980. Swaziland would become independent in 1968, but all the other countries she visited had gained their independence recently, between 1960 and 1964.

Chapter 6

Wally watched Apollo 5 take off from the Cape Kennedy Air Force Station in Florida. That launch facility had opened in 1950 with the name Cape Canaveral but was renamed in 1963 in honor of the recently assassinated President. The name of the facility returned to its original designation in 1973 and has been Cape Canaveral since then.

The final two human Moon landings, Apollo 16 and Apollo 17, took place in roughly the first year that Wally worked for the FAA. Manned spaceflights tapered off rapidly after that. One highlight was the Apollo-Soyuz Test Project in July 1975, a month after Wally attended the White House brunch as an investigator for the NTSB. That joint project of the Soviet and American space programs involved the docking of their respective crewed spacecraft in Earth orbit. Three astronauts and two cosmonauts occupied the connected vehicles for nearly two days, conducting cooperative experiments.

NASA's next crewed spacecraft program began in April 1981 with the first space shuttle mission, a two-day flight in Earth orbit. Seventeen more space shuttle missions took place before Wally left the NTSB in May 1985, including Sally Ride's two flights as the first American female astronaut in June 1983 and October 1984. Kathryn Sullivan, another American woman, was on that second flight, and she took the first female EVA (spacewalk) in history.

The first space shuttle disaster, the explosion of the *Challenger* shortly after it lifted off from Cape Canaveral in January 1986, happened eight months after Wally left the NTSB. Two women were on board that flight. It was the second spaceflight for Judy Resnik, one of the first group of women selected to be NASA astronauts. Christa McAuliffe, a high school social studies teacher, became the first civilian to die in a space accident.

Chapter 7

Like Wally, several of the other Mercury 13 participated in the Civil Air Patrol, as students, pilots, and/or instructors.

Chapter 8

You can see Wally in action, teaching pilots how to conduct a proper preflight inspection online at youtube.com/watch?v=d6A8chppAe0. She recorded this video when she was working for the NTSB between 1975 and 1985.

Chapter 9

The travels Wally described in this chapter took place between 1977 and 1988. International politics were complex during that period, with ongoing Cold War tensions between the free West and the communist countries of China and the Soviet Union. For example, her visit to China in 1987 came four months after a series of student demonstrations seeking political reforms. About a year after her visit, a series of pro-democracy demonstrations began in Beijing's Tiananmen Square. In June 1989, the final demonstration was quashed when government troops in armored vehicles fired on the demonstrators, killing hundreds of them.

Her group's visit to Moscow in 1988 came at the conclusion of a summit conference between U.S. President Ronald Reagan and Soviet leader Mikhail Gorbachev when they finalized a nuclear arms treaty and discussed human rights issues.

The Mir space station Wally mentioned was the first modular space station and was designed for long-term research with continuous occupation. The first crew of two cosmonauts lived on it for seventy-five days in 1986. Then it remained unmanned for nearly seven months before the second module was added in 1987. It was occupied by three cosmonauts during Wally's 1988 visit to the Soviet Union.

Chapter 10

Eventually, the U.S. military branches allowed women to be trained and serve as pilots—the Navy in 1973, the Army in 1974, and the Air Force in 1976. They didn't admit women to their test pilot schools until a decade later. In 1978, NASA accepted the first women astronauts—six of them in a group of thirty-three new space crew members. When Sally Ride became America's first woman in space in 1983, she politely endured reporters' gender-based questions. Sometimes she simply didn't answer, but once she commented, "It may be too bad that our society isn't further along and that this is such a big deal."

Wally's deep and enduring interest in crewed spaceflight is reflected in a collection of *Life* and *Time* magazines she has kept. Twenty-seven issues in all, they date from August 29, 1960, to December 12, 1969. *Life* was a large-format (ten and a half inches by thirteen and three-fourths inches) publication that included numerous, large photographs with each article. Here is a chronological summary:

In the only issue Wally kept from 1960, *Life* described Jerrie Cobb's astronaut-type physical exams at the Lovelace Clinic. Those tests had been done that year, when Cobb was twenty-nine years old and had 7,500 hours of flying time in aircraft ranging from crop dusters to B-17s. The magazine brought Cobb back to Albuquerque to photograph reenactments of some of her tests. The article dubbed her "Space Lady."

Life's January 27, 1961, issue featured the inauguration of President John F. Kennedy on the cover. Inside was a story written by John Glenn. The Mercury astronauts had an exclusive contract with *Life* to report on their personal and professional lives. Glenn's article, "We're Going Places No One Has Ever Traveled in a Craft No One's Flown," described the recent, successful test flight of the Mercury spacecraft and Redstone launch vehicle. A few days later, a similar test would carry the chimpanzee Ham on a flight to verify the life-support systems and the ability of the human surrogate to perform during suborbital flight. One photograph showed Glenn preparing for possible disorientation during spaceflight by tossing tennis balls into a waste basket inside a chamber that was spinning ten times per minute.

The February 10, 1961, issue of *Life* reported on Ham's test flight. The article also described the training program for about twenty other chimpanzees who had been Ham's classmates at Holloman Air Force Base in Alamogordo, New Mexico. One of them, named Enos, would take an orbital test flight in late

November 1961 before NASA sent its first human into orbit.

John Glenn, Gus Grissom, and Alan Shepard appeared on the cover of the March 3, 1961, issue of *Life*. One of them would be chosen to take the first manned, suborbital flight of the Mercury program. The article emphasized the astronauts' roles as husbands and fathers. One photo showed Glenn, wearing "his wife's apron," shaping hamburger patties with the help of his daughter. Another showed Grissom patching a leak on the roof of his home. Two photos of Shepard showed him inspecting the engine in his Corvette and clowning during an astronaut group photo session.

Wally had tucked two clippings inside that magazine. One was a page from the March 3, 1961, issue of *Time*, with a cartoon showing Ham instructing Grissom, Glenn, and Shepard about flying a spacecraft. All seven of the astronauts had been chagrinned to be preceded in flight by a chimpanzee. In the cartoon, Ham said, "… then, at 900,000 feet, you'll get the feeling that you *must* have a banana!"

The other clipping was an article from the February 26, 1961, issue of *Parade* magazine that speculated on the construction of the first American base on the Moon, based on plans developed by the U.S. Army Corps of Engineers. The article speculated that the first two men to land on the Moon would be a physician, who would also serve as a welder and dietician, and a scientist-engineer, who would also act as a radio operator and bulldozer driver.

The April 21, 1961, issues of both *Time* and *Life* reported on the first man in space, Yuri Gagarin. The Russian cosmonaut had flown one orbit on April 12. Both magazines also reported on the war crimes trial of former Nazi official Adolph Eichmann.

Three weeks later, on May 12, both magazines featured the suborbital flight of Alan Shepard, America's first man in space. His flight had lasted fifteen minutes. *Life* also ran an article written by Shepard's wife describing their family's experiences during the flight and the week leading up to it.

The following week's issue of *Life* included an eight-page article in which Shepard described his experience. During the flight, he had taken over manual control from the autopilot, one axis at a time—pointing the capsule up or down, left or right, and rotating clockwise or counterclockwise. Then he brought the capsule to its reentry attitude before switching back to autopilot for the landing. Gagarin's flight had not involved any manual control of his spacecraft.

The March 2, 1962, issues of both magazines featured America's first manned orbital flight performed on February 20. The three-orbit mission lasted 115 minutes. The *Time* reporter wrote, "In terms of national prestige, Glenn's flight put the U.S. back in the space race with a vengeance, and gave the morale of the U.S. and the entire free world a huge and badly needed boost." After America's second manned suborbital flight in July 1961, Russian cosmonaut Gherman Titov had spent twenty-five hours in space on a seventeen-orbit mission in August 1961.

The March 9, 1962, issue of *Life* ran Glenn's seven-page article describing his orbital flight. He wrote that his post-flight debriefing included a session with the astronauts' staff psychiatrist, Dr. George Ruff. Glenn filled out a questionnaire that was routinely used after training and practice sessions. The last question asked whether there was any unusual activity during the session. He wrote, "I couldn't resist it. 'No,' I wrote, 'just a normal day in space.'"

Life's April 27, 1962, cover showed a man testing a lunar EVA suit that looks strange by today's standards. The body and helmet were rigid material, while the accordion-pleated arms and legs allowed some flexibility. The accompanying article, "Our Next Goal: Man on the Moon," described preparations for the Apollo program and its three-man spacecraft designed to visit the Moon. The article also described the soon-to-be-launched Gemini program, in which two astronauts in Earth orbit would test equipment and procedures for EVAs and in-orbit docking of two spacecraft. Those activities would be necessary for landing humans on the Moon.

On May 18, 1962, *Life* featured Scott Carpenter and his wife, Rene. Carpenter would take the next Mercury flight of three Earth orbits the following week. The profile traced his growth from a "boyhood full of roaming and recklessness" to that of a "quiet man" and father of four.

Two weeks later, *Life's* June 1 issue carried an article in which Rene Carpenter described her family's reactions during her husband's May 24 flight. A series of photos showed her in deep concern as his flight ended. He had overshot the landing site by more than 200 miles, and the Navy recovery team didn't locate him for forty minutes. The next photo showed her jubilation as she learned he was being picked up from the Atlantic Ocean.

Carpenter's own recollections of his flight appeared in the June 8, 1962, issue of *Life*. He was candid in describing his emotions during and after the flight. He wrote that as he floated in his life raft awaiting the recovery team, he "sat for a long time just thinking about what I'd been through…. I had made mistakes and some things had gone wrong, but other men could learn from my experiences."

Next in Wally's stack of magazines is an August 10, 1962, issue of *Time*. A six-page article detailed plans for NASA's ultimate objective of landing men on the Moon. Two diagrams explained the operations that would be involved in a lunar orbit rendezvous, which had recently become the preferred option for Moon trips. It meant sending a two-part spacecraft into lunar orbit and detaching the landing module to carry two of the three crewmen to the surface. After their explorations, the two men would reenter the landing module, which would blast them back up to rejoin the orbiting command module.

The May 24, 1963, issues of both magazines carried lengthy stories about Gordon Cooper's May 15 twenty-two-orbit flight. The last of the Mercury program missions, it lasted more than thirty-four hours. *Time* emphasized the perilous part of the flight, when the autopilot system failed just before the spacecraft began its reentry into the atmosphere. "[Cooper] had to respond with incredible precision to directions from [Glenn in Mission Control]; he had to show a kind of skill and nerve and calm that no man has ever had to demonstrate. While people around the world listened with deep anxiety, Major Cooper seemed cooler than any man on earth." *Life,* on the other hand, ran a long companion story about Einstein's theory of relativity and how it meant that during Cooper's spaceflight, he aged twenty-two millionths of a second less than he would have on Earth. That issue of *Life* also contained a story about the first James Bond movie, *Dr. No* starring Sean Connery as 007.

In the following week's issue of *Life,* Gordon Cooper's wife, Trudy, wrote about her experiences during his spaceflight. That issue also included a story about the Black Muslims, "a Negro sect which preaches that whites are devils and takes on new prominence in a time of racial impatience and violence. And a Negro photographer, Gordon Parks, permitted inside the secretive movement, explains in a moving article 'What their cry means to me.'"

Coverage of the racial unrest in America continued in the June 28, 1963, issue of *Life,* which carried a cover photo of the widow and son of Medgar Evers. Evers, a black man who worked for the NAACP (National Association for the Advancement of Colored People) and was murdered in Mississippi, was buried at Arlington National Cemetery in Washington, D.C. The same issue contained an article about female cosmonaut Valentina Tereshkova's forty-eight-orbit flight that lasted twenty-three hours. An accompanying article was written by Clare Booth Luce, a prominent journalist and the first American woman appointed to a major ambassadorial post. A former member of the U.S. House of Representatives, she had served as ambassador to Brazil and Italy during President Dwight Eisenhower's two terms. In the article titled "But Some People Simply Never Get the Message," Luce outlined how America could have sent the first woman into space, referring to the Mercury 13, all of whose photographs were included.

Life's September 27, 1963, cover story was about the next nine astronauts chosen by NASA for the Gemini program. It described some of the training activities the nine new men along with the Mercury 7 were using to prepare for their upcoming missions. A second article featured photographs and brief descriptions of their wives and children. Another brief article showed special tools that were developed for use in space, including a "plench" (combination pliers and wrench) and a "hand zert" (a zero-reaction hand-held tool with which an astronaut turned a bolt by squeezing two handles rather than twisting).

Then Wally's magazine collection jumps to the Apollo program with the July 4, 1969, issue of *Life*. One article profiled the three astronauts who would make the first human landing trip to the Moon in the Apollo 11 mission: Neil Armstrong, Buzz Aldrin, and Mike Collins. Another article described how the flight would proceed, and a third article described the new laboratory where the lunar samples brought back by the astronauts would be stored and examined. Finally, the issue included a letter from Charles Lindbergh, a pilot who had made the first nonstop airplane flight from New York to Paris forty-two years earlier. He mentioned how he had assisted Robert Goddard's work on liquid-fuel rockets in the 1930s. He also wrote about watching the launch of Apollo 8, which in December 1968 had flown a crew of three to lunar orbit and then back to Earth. "I was literally hypnotized by the launching," Lindbergh wrote. "I have spent most of a lifetime in close contact with test flying and man-controlled power; but I have never experienced anything to compare to that mission of Apollo 8."

The July 25, 1969, issue of *Life* also featured the Apollo 11 mission. It had launched on July 16 and gone into lunar orbit on July 19. Armstrong and Aldrin landed on the Moon on July 20. Mike Collins spent twenty-eight hours alone in lunar orbit while the others descended to the surface, explored, deployed experiments, and returned to orbit for docking with the command module. They all returned to Earth on July 24. *Life* showed small images of its thirty-two issues between 1959 and 1969 that featured cover stories about America's manned space programs.

Tucked inside that issue of *Life* were several pages Wally saved from the August 1, 1969, issue of the *Los Angeles Times* with eight pictures the astronauts took during their EVA on the Moon's surface. Another article showed photographs of Mars taken by the unmanned spacecraft Mariner 6. The headline of an accompanying article read, "Manned Two-Year Mars Trip Believed Possible by 1981." Another front-page story in that paper was about President Richard Nixon's administration's willingness to accept the division of Vietnam into North and South countries in order to end the unpopular war.

The August 8, 1969, issue of *Life* ran thirteen pages of photos and descriptions of the Apollo 11 mission by Armstrong and Aldrin. Another photo essay in that issue explored the Watergate, a co-op apartment and office complex in Washington, D.C., that had become the fashionable place to live during the administration of President Richard Nixon. That complex would later play a key role in Nixon's 1974 resignation from the Presidency.

Life published a special edition on August 8, 1969, titled *To the Moon and Back*. It was completely devoted to the Apollo 11 mission and the astronauts who flew it.

The last issue in Wally's collection is the December 12, 1969, issue of *Life*. The cover story was the second human landing on the Moon, Apollo 12. On that mission, astronauts Pete Conrad and Alan Bean landed right on target, about 600 feet from the unmanned *Surveyor* spacecraft that had made a soft landing on the Moon two and a half years earlier. They examined it and brought back some of its parts so scientists could evaluate how various materials had withstood exposure to the lunar environment.

Chapter 11

The Ansari X Prize was inspired by the Orteig Prize that Charles Lindbergh won in 1927 with his nonstop airplane flight from New York to Paris. Raymond Orteig, a New York hotel owner, offered a $25,000 prize for that feat in order to encourage the development of aviation. In 1994, a student pilot named Peter Diamandis read about that and decided to create a similar contest to encourage the development of a commercial space industry. Nine teams attempted to win the Orteig Prize between its announcement in May 1919 and Lindbergh's success eight years later. Diamandis announced the X Prize competition in May 1996. Of the twenty-six teams that signed up to participate, the first to actually attempt the required flights succeeded in October 2004.

Wally Funk

The Mercury 13

This book has been about one of the Mercury 13, Wally Funk, with a couple of others mentioned briefly. Here is a summary of the other twelve members of the group and what they did after the program ended:

Jerrie Cobb was in many ways a leader of the group, much to the consternation of Jackie Cochran, who helped Dr. Lovelace organize the program and provided much of the financial support for it. After her efforts failed to keep the Women in Space program alive, Cobb spent most of her life in South America flying supplies to communities of indigenous people in the Amazon jungle. She died in 2019.

Myrtle "K" Cagle married a former flying student in 1960. She wore a wedding gown made of parachutes. She later became licensed as an airframe and power plant airplane mechanic and worked at Robins Air Force Base in Georgia. Once, she was invited to visit Eglin Air Force Base in Florida by an Air Force general she interviewed for a newspaper column she was writing. On that 1953 visit, she was allowed to fly a T-33 jet airplane—a rare opportunity for a woman. She died in 2019.

Jan Dietrich had been a chief pilot for two flight schools, a test pilot for multi-engine aircraft for Cessna, and a pilot examiner for the FAA prior to her Lovelace testing. Later, during the Vietnam War, she worked for World Airways, a military contractor, flying regularly between its base in Oakland and the war zone. She stopped flying after the 1974 death of her twin sister, Marion. Jan died in 2008.

Marion Dietrich, Jan's twin sister, was a newspaper reporter as well as a commercial transport pilot who flew charter and ferry flights. After the Lovelace testing, the Dietrichs became allies of Jackie Cochran in opposing the Mercury 13 leadership of Jerrie Cobb. Marion died of cancer.

Sarah Gorelick (later **Ratley**) had a degree in mathematics and had worked for AT&T as an engineer. In later years, she became a certified public accountant and worked for the IRS. Her flying was personal and recreational. She died in 2020.

Jane Hart was a helicopter pilot as well as an airplane pilot. She sometimes flew her husband, Senator Philip Hart, to speaking engagements when he was campaigning. She developed a friendship with feminist Betty Friedan and was a founding member of the National Organization for Women (NOW). During the administration of President Lyndon Johnson, Hart chaired the Women's Advisory Committee on Aviation for the FAA. She died in 2015.

Jean Hixson was a member of the Women Airforce Service Pilots (WASPs) during World War II, flying various types of noncombat missions including delivering aircraft to war zones. After the Lovelace testing, she joined the Air Force Reserves and worked on research projects involving space navigation and movement in reduced gravity during the Apollo era and beyond. She retired from the Air Force Reserves as a full colonel in 1982 and died in 1984.

Rhea Hurrle (later **Woltman),** a charter pilot, was one of only three of the Mercury 13 to take another type of astronaut qualification test, namely the isolation tank test that Cobb and Funk both took. Afterward, she helped with instruction at the Air Force Academy in Colorado. In 1972, she married and, without regret, stopped flying at the request of her new husband. She became a professional parliamentarian.

Irene Leverton worked for a flight school that also flew Hollywood celebrities on air taxi flights. She took unauthorized time off for the abruptly cancelled Pensacola tests, and when she went back to work found her duties had been reduced to instructing beginning students. She later became an FAA certificated Airline Transport Pilot and served as a check pilot for a Civil Air Patrol squadron in Arizona. She died in 2017.

Jerri Sloan (later **Truhill**) co-owned a flying service that conducted equipment test flights for Texas Instruments and for the U.S. military. She served on the board of directors for the International Women's Air and Space Museum and became an active advocate for women's rights, particularly in aviation and aerospace. She died in 2013.

Bernice "B" Steadman owned her own aviation business, including an air taxi service, when she took part in the Lovelace tests. Later, she served as president of the Ninety-Nines and was a co-founder of the International Women's Air and Space Museum in Ohio. After suffering a brain injury in the 1970s, she stopped flying but continued to speak about careers in aviation and space. She died in 2015.

Gene Nora Stumbough (later **Jessen**) was teaching at Oklahoma State University when she applied for the Lovelace tests. Because the Pensacola tests would take place after the next semester started, she quit her job. Afterward, she found work as a flight instructor before becoming a sales demonstration pilot for Beechcraft airplanes. She later served as president of the Ninety-Nines and helped found the Ninety-Nines Museum of Women Pilots.

Wally Funk

Resources

Air Race Classic: Women's air racing started in 1929 with the Women's Air Derby. Twenty pilots raced from Santa Monica, CA to Cleveland, OH, the site of the National Air Races. Racing continued through the 1930s and was renewed again after WWII when the All Women's Transcontinental Air Race (AWTAR), better known as the Powder Puff Derby, came into being in 1947. The AWTAR held its 30th, final, and commemorative flight in 1977. When the AWTAR was discontinued, the Air Race Classic (ARC) stepped in to continue the tradition of transcontinental speed competition for women pilots and staged its premier race. https://www.airraceclassic.org

All-American Girls Professional Baseball League: The AAGPBL Players Association is a non-profit organization dedicated to preserving the History of the AAGPBL and supporting women and girls all across our country who deserve the opportunity to play "Hardball." https://www.aagpbl.org

Association for Women in Aviation Maintenance: AWAM is a nonprofit organization formed for the purpose of championing women's professional growth and enrichment in aviation maintenance by providing opportunities for sharing information, networking, education, fostering a sense of community, and increasing public awareness of women in the industry. https://www.awam.org

Fédération Aéronautique Internationale: The Fédération Aéronautique Internationale, FAI, the World Air Sports Federation, was founded in 1905. It is a non-governmental and non-profit making international organization with the basic aim of furthering aeronautical and astronautical activities worldwide, ratifying world and continental records, and coordinating the organization of international competitions. It is recognized by the International Olympic Committee (IOC). https://www.fai.org

International Forest of Friendship: The International Forest of Friendship is a living, growing memorial to the world history of aviation and aerospace. The Forest was a gift to America on Amelia Earhart's 200th birthday in 1976 from the City of Atchison, Kansas (her birthplace); the Ninety-Nines (International Organization of Women Pilots); and the Kansas State University, Kansas Forest Service. https://ifof.org

National Intercollegiate Flying Association: The National Intercollegiate Flying Association (NIFA) was formed for the purposes of developing and advancing aviation education; to promote, encourage, and foster safety in aviation; to promote and foster communications and cooperation between aviation students, educators, educational institutions, and the aviation industry; and to provide an arena for collegiate aviation competition. https://nifa.aero

Ninety-Nines: The Ninety-Nines, Inc., is an international organization of licensed women pilots from 44 countries. https://www.ninety-nines.org

Single Action Shooting Society: The Single Action Shooting Society is an international organization created to preserve and promote the sport of Cowboy Action Shooting. SASS endorses regional matches conducted by affiliated clubs, stages END of TRAIL (the World Championship of Cowboy Action Shooting), promulgates rules and procedures to ensure safety and consistency in Cowboy Action Shooting matches, and seeks to protect its members' 2nd Amendment rights. https://sassnet.com

Women in Aviation International: Women in Aviation International (WAI) is a nonprofit organization dedicated to the encouragement and advancement of women in all aviation career fields and interests. https://www.wai.org

Women in Military Service For America Memorial: The Women in Military Service For America Memorial, at the Ceremonial Entrance to Arlington National Cemetery, is the only major national memorial honoring all women who have defended America throughout history. https://www.womensmemorial.org

Zonta International: Zonta International is a leading global organization of professionals empowering women worldwide through service and advocacy. https://www.zonta.org

Wally Funk

Index

A

accident investigation 98, 138, 239
air races 239
Alabama 176, 239
Albuquerque, New Mexico 16, 34, 209
Aldrin, Buzz 176, 201, 221, 222
Ansari, Anousheh 191, 196
Ansari X Prize 196, 198, 199, 223
Apollo program 218, 221
Australia 195
Austria 71, 72, 73

B

Belgium 67, 71
Broadwick, Tiny 175, 176

C

Cagle, Myrtle 225
California 4, 59, 62, 64, 67, 82, 87, 89, 90, 91, 92, 94, 96, 101, 106, 113, 114, 120, 121, 124, 126, 131, 133, 148, 157, 159, 182, 185, 197, 205
Cape Canaveral 180, 213, 214
Carpenter, Scott 175, 176, 211, 212, 219
centrifuge 64, 65, 177, 185, 186
China 8, 156, 159, 161, 162, 163, 164, 165, 166, 215
Civil Air Patrol 114, 115, 214, 227
Cochran, Jackie 36, 49, 51, 58, 211, 225, 226

Collins, Eileen 1, 9, 13, 178, 179, 180, 181, 182, 183, 239
Colorado 14, 118, 123, 175, 226
Cooper, Gordon 67, 176, 211, 220
Creasy, Tower 24
Czechoslovakia 73, 74

D

Dateline (NBC) 65, 179, 211
Deshmukh, Saudamini (Minoo) 157
Dietrich, Jan 49, 225, 226
Dietrich, Marion 49, 225, 226

E

Earhart, Amelia 23, 26, 148, 150, 230
Egypt 77, 78, 213
Eisenhower, Dwight 13, 209, 221
El Toro Marine Corps Air Station 62
Emery Flight School 118, 119, 122, 175
England 71, 83, 126, 128, 170, 171, 191

F

FAA 8, 36, 91, 92, 93, 94, 96, 107, 119, 121, 133, 137, 139, 146, 148, 174, 213, 225, 226, 227
Federal Aviation Administration 91
Florida 21, 48, 89, 90, 96, 119, 126, 211, 213, 225
Flying Aggies 25, 26, 28, 30, 149
Flying Susies 24
Fort Sill 31, 33, 35, 36, 47, 51, 57, 62, 98, 133
France 68, 70, 71, 129, 191
Friedan, Betty 226
Funk, Lozier 8 (see also Father)
Funk, Virginia Shy 8 (see also Mother)

G

Gagarin, Yuri 185, 193, 217, 218
Gemini program 210, 219, 221
Germany 27, 70, 71, 129, 191
Glenn, John 13, 57, 92, 174, 183, 211, 212, 216, 217, 218, 220
glider 27, 31, 90, 91, 128

Gorbachev, Mikhail 165, 215
Gorelick, Sarah (later Ratley) 226
Greece 75, 78

H

Hart, Janey 58, 211
helicopter 95, 97, 98, 102, 103, 105, 118, 134, 142, 151, 226
high-altitude chamber 62, 63
Hixson, Jean 226
Hurrle, Rhea (later Woltman) 52, 226

I

India 8, 153, 156, 157, 158
Interorbital Systems 195, 196, 197
isolation test 57
Israel 86, 87
Italy 70, 71, 78, 221

K

Kilgore, Dr. Donald 16, 46, 179
Korzun, Valery 190

L

Lapsley, Tiner 26, 27
Leverton, Irene 227
Life magazine 33, 54
Los Alamos National Laboratory 42, 43
Los Alamos, New Mexico 42, 43
Lovelace Clinic 6, 16, 36, 37, 43, 46, 48, 51, 52, 174, 175, 176, 179, 209, 210, 216
Lovelace, Dr. William Randolph (Randy) II 209

M

Man in Space Soonest program 208
Martin-Baker ejection seat test. 62
Mercury 7 11, 16, 48, 175, 176, 183, 221
Mercury 13 4, 9, 11, 12, 13, 16, 48, 52, 58, 59, 137, 166, 173, 179, 180, 183, 191, 211, 212, 214, 221, 225, 226, 243
Mercury program 217, 220

Mike Douglas Show 174, 175
Milliron, Randa 195, 196, 197, 198
Milliron, Rod 195
Mir space station 168, 185, 189, 215
Morocco 78, 79, 213

N

NASA 11, 13, 16, 17, 33, 35, 38, 47, 58, 59, 65, 89, 142, 146, 173, 174, 175, 176, 178, 179, 180, 182, 183, 191, 195, 208, 209, 210, 211, 214, 215, 217, 219, 221
National Air Races 229
National Intercollegiate Flying Association (NIFA) 24, 149, 230
National Transportation Safety Board 12, 93, 96
Ninety-Nines 25, 30, 34, 52, 120, 124, 148, 149, 153, 157, 159, 165, 169, 179, 227, 230

O

O'Keeffe, Georgia 6, 169, 207
Oklahoma 25, 26, 27, 28, 31, 34, 52, 90, 92, 93, 148, 149, 179, 208, 227, 243
Oklahoma State University 25, 149, 208, 227, 243

P

parachute 94, 95, 175, 176, 187
Portugal 69, 79, 213
Powder Puff Derby 122, 123, 125, 229
PSA Airlines Boeing 727 107

R

Reagan, Ronald 165, 215
Ride, Sally 166, 174, 214, 215
Rolls Royce 126, 127, 128, 129, 130
Russia 8, 72, 73, 74, 165, 167, 169, 184, 193
Rwanda 85

S

Shurley, Dr. Jay T. 34
Single Action Shooting Society 131, 231

Sloan, Jerri (later Truhill) 227
South Africa 79, 80, 81, 82, 154, 213
Space Academy 176, 184
Space Adventures 9, 193
Space Cruiser System 194, 198
Spaceport America 200, 203
space shuttle 11, 13, 166, 174, 177, 178, 180, 182, 204, 205, 214
Spain 69
Steadman, Bernice 227
Stephens College 7, 14, 17
Stumbough, Gene Nora (later Jessen) 52, 227
Switzerland 70, 71, 87, 129
Syria 76, 87

T

Tanzania 83, 84, 85
Taos, New Mexico 114
Tereshkovam, Valentina 65, 72, 165, 167, 212, 220
Texas 6, 96, 117, 119, 131, 133, 136, 170, 191, 197, 227
Tonga 195
Travel Channel 184, 193
Trout, Bobbi 23, 205

U

University of Southern California 64, 185

V

Virgin Galactic 9, 13, 199, 200, 202, 203

W

Wally stick 8, 137, 138
Warner, Emily Howell 121
Willard, Charles 176
Women in Aviation International 150, 178, 183, 231, 243
Wright's Flying Service 59, 60, 67, 90

Wally Funk

About the Authors

Loretta Hall has been intrigued with human spaceflight since her adolescent years. She followed the progress of the Mercury, Gemini, and Apollo missions and was thrilled to watch the first human steps on the Moon in 1969. The images on her black-and-white television screen were grainy and almost ghostlike, but the accomplishment was clear.

Loretta shared this fascination with millions of people around the world, including Wally Funk. Wally is a visual person, and she even took snapshot photos of her television screen showing the first Moonwalkers.

Wally and Loretta didn't meet until nearly fifty years later, but they quickly became friends. By this time, Loretta had become a freelance writer and had written eight books, half of them about space exploration. Wally had decided it was time to record her life story in book form. The partnership was natural.

Another thing Loretta and Wally have in common is a love of New Mexico. In 1977, Loretta and her husband, Jerry Hall, moved to Albuquerque. They raised their three daughters there and put down deep roots. Wally was born and raised in northern New Mexico and has always regarded the state as her physical and emotional home.

Loretta is active in the writing and space communities. She has served as an elected officer for six years in New

Mexico Press Women and was named 2016 Communicator of Achievement by the National Federation of Press Women. She is a subcommittee chair and a Certified Space Ambassador for the National Space Society.

You can find out more about Wally and Loretta and contact them through their websites: WallyFly.com and AuthorHall.com.

Wally's Awards
A Partial List

Adler Planetarium's Women in Space Science Award (Mercury 13)

Daughters of the American Revolution's Excellence in Community Service Award

Delta Airlines Wall of Honor

International Forest of Friendship Honoree

Smithsonian National Air & Space Museum Wall of Honor

Veterans of Foreign Wars of the United States Aeronautics and Aerospace Gold Medal

Pratt & Whitney Aviation Pioneer Award

Oklahoma State University's Aviation Hall of Fame

U.S. Space & Rocket Center's Space Camp Hall of Fame

Women in Aviation International's Pioneer Hall of Fame

Women in Aviation International's 100 Most Influential Women in the Aviation and Aerospace Industry

Wally Funk

Higher Faster Longer

ORDERING BOOKS
FOR QUANTITY SALES

Special discounts are available on quantity purchases by corporations, associations, and others. For details, contact the author's publicist at the following URL: *www.wallyfly.com/ContactWally.html*